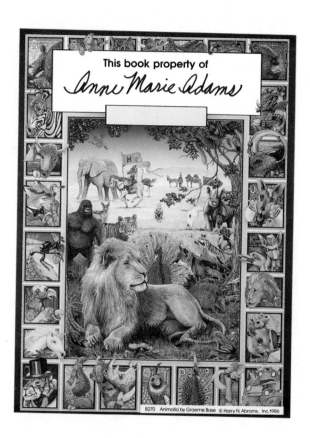

This book property of

Anne Marie Adams

B270 Animalia by Graeme Base © Harry N. Abrams, Inc.1986

IN SEARCH OF YOURSELF

The Beginning

JANET DIAN

Illustrated by Lena Hardt

Expansions Publishing Company, Inc.

Expansions Publishing
609 W. Washington St. 11-54
Sequim, WA 98382

Other books by Janet Dian —
In Search of Yourself: Moving Forward

Library of Congress Catalog Card Number: 90-81726

ISBN 0-9626446-0-9

First Printing 1990
Second Printing 1991

Publisher's Cataloging in Publication

Dian, Janet
   In search of yourself : the beginning / Janet Dian. --
   p. cm. -- (Self-healing through self-awareness ; book 1)
   Includes index.
   ISBN 0-9626446-0-9 (pbk.)

   1. Metaphysics. 2. Self-realization. 3. Parapsychology.
I. Title. II. Series.

BP605.N48   133

                     90-81726

A
SERIES
ON
SELF-HEALING
THROUGH
SELF-AWARENESS

Book 1

*TO MY FAMILY
AND MY EXTENDED FAMILY*

CONTENTS

INTRODUCTION

Dear Friends,

I have been involved in the process of self-healing through self-awareness all my life. Because I was raised in "new thought", I learned to question and evaluate myself at a very young age.

I not only questioned myself, I questioned everything. As I got older, I realized that the principles I had been taught were a good starting point, but I needed more in order to have peace within myself and my life.

As I learned about myself, I found that I could share my learning with others. Most people could use the same tools and principles that helped me, with the same basic results—they became more peaceful inside, and as a result, their outer world flowed smoother.

I have watched my students promote their own self-healing through inner awareness. I have seen them heal their bodies, minds, and spirituality. It is because of their willingness to work with these tools and principles that this book has been written.

I teach my students to be skeptical, to always question, and to test the tools and principles for their validity. My only request is that they keep an open mind and meditate for five minutes every day. I encourage them to utilize what they can, and to discard the rest; to expand upon what works for them; and to add their own individuality wherever possible. I ask the same of you.

In this book I share with you some of these tools and principles. As you use them, you will find them automatically becoming a part of your daily living because they make you feel better and your life flow smoother. Use these tools as the catalyst that promotes your own inner healing.

Inner healing can begin now, wherever you are in your life. New concepts prepare you for alternative avenues of action that can filter into your conscious mind. New solutions to old challenges can now come forward.

Join me now as I walk you through this path of self-awareness.

Wishing you inner peace,

Janet Dian

Janet Dian

SLOWING DOWN

Hidden within every moment of your life are all the answers that you will ever need. All you have to do is slow down long enough to let your moments teach you. Within each one, you state who and what you are. Within each one, your outer world reflects that statement back to you.

You may label your present moment very ordinary and mundane, but it is actually full of information that can take you into a whole new path of inner awareness. Each moment contains many, many clues that tell you who you are. Find your own clues *right now*.

Body Language

How are you sitting? Why did you choose that position? What inner thoughts and feelings are you expressing through your body language? Are you:

relaxed?

open and receptive?

open and skeptical?

closed and skeptical?

closed and uninterested?

tense?

Clothing

What clothes are you wearing? Why did you choose them? What do they express about your inner self? Are they:

dark and gloomy?

dark and grounding?

light and freeing?

light and spacy?

patterned and too busy?

striped and running you around in circles?

solid and strong?

solid and inflexible?

plaid and breaking up old patterns?

balanced or unbalanced?

Colors

What colors are you wearing? What do they tell you about your inner self? Are you wearing:

green because it is a healing color, or because you are envious and jealous?

18

blue because it is calming, or because you are depressed?

yellow because you are wise, or because you are fearful?

brown because it is grounding, or because your thinking is muddy?

red because you are creative, or because you are angry?

purple because you are spiritual, or because you are selfish?

Your Home

What room are you in? What does it tell you about your inner self? Does it:

promote openness and communication?

promote privacy?

establish barriers?

feel comfortable and warm?

feel distant and cold?

Is the room in order?

Is it full of clutter?

This may reflect a mind that is full of clutter.

Does it have closets and drawers that you think need to be cleaned out?

This may reflect a mind that is ready to let go of the past.

Does everything *have* to be in its place?

This may reflect a mind that is strict and inflexible.

Is there any dust?

19

This may reflect a mind that is afraid to let go of the past.

Are there any cobwebs?

This may reflect a mind that needs some mental exercise.

A Myriad Of Clues

By slowing down for just a few seconds, you have already found a myriad of clues that tell you who and what you are. When you take the time to stop and look around, you can find many more clues.

The way that you dress, the colors that you choose, the way you wear your hair, the arrangement of furniture and light in your home, the food that you eat, your yard, and your car are all clues that lead you into yourself.

Yes, they are very ordinary, but when you take the time to understand them, they become very interesting. Understanding them means understanding another level of yourself.

Understanding Your Now

Remember when you were in school learning math? First, you learned to add and subtract. *Then* you learned to multiply and divide. You built one concept upon the other. In the same way, understanding what is happening *right now* is the first concept that you need. *Then*, you can understand the moment before the moment, or the moment after the moment.

Your present moment always holds the key to your past and future. Whatever you choose to express *right now* is a result of your past actions. Whatever you choose to express *right now* also sets your future in motion.

Whenever you have a question, look at your present moment. You will always find a clue that will lead you into an answer. Initially the clue may appear minute or insignificant, but it will direct you if you let it.

Learning from your present moment slows you down, helping you to stop and think before you act. It also teaches you to find your own answers, establishing a healthy, firm foundation upon which to build and grow.

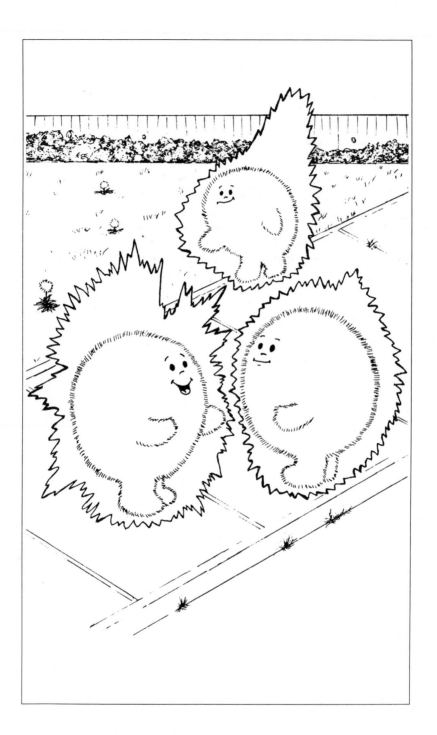

DEFINING YOUR SPACE

Your own personal space consists of the area around you that contains who and what you are. This is your own personal energy field, more commonly referred to as your "aura." The basic shape of an aura is an oval, but there are as many variations on the shape as there are people.

For example, auras can be:

Lop-sided.

Long and skinny.

Short and fat.

Very narrow and close to the body.

Very wide and shooting out far from the body.

Close to the body and shooting out in some places.

Close to the body on the bottom and wide on top.

Very narrow on top and wide on the bottom.

This gives you an idea of some basic variations. One variation is not "better" than another; each merely is an expression of a unique individual. The shape of your aura changes depending upon the experiences that you are going through at any particular time. Your aura can even change from day to day. As you grow, it goes through many changes.

Feeling Your Aura

Determine the shape of your own aura by feeling it. Starting at your feet, move up your body with your thoughts. Feel how far out it goes, and how far up. Feel the space inside of your aura. Then, feel the space outside of your aura. You will be able to feel a difference.

The space inside of your aura feels like you. The space outside of your aura does not. On some level, you have always been aware of the shape of your aura. You are just taking the time to bring that awareness into your conscious mind.

Mixing Auras

You can also tell when your aura is mixing with someone else's. For example, if someone stands too close to you, you say that they are in your "space." You feel his/her aura mixing with your own. It makes you uncomfortable and you feel an invasion of your privacy. You intuitively want to take a couple of steps back to keep your auras separate.

Taking a couple of steps back will not always help. For instance, your aura may have places where it shoots out six feet from you. Or, you may be around someone whose aura shoots out six feet toward you. Taking a couple of steps back will not change anything. Furthermore, taking a couple of steps back is not always possible. You may find yourself at a crowded meeting or in the middle of a crowded shopping mall. In close quarters, you may feel uncomfortable without knowing why. The reason is because you mix auras with other people without being aware that this is happening.

Their auras are in your aura, and on some level of awareness you feel whatever is going on in their lives. Because most people try to express positive aspects while suppressing negative ones, negative feelings are often the most prominent in auras.

For example, on some level you feel the mood swings, relationships, financial status, home life, occupation, and stresses, as well as all the other feelings that surround them.

Whatever others feel may directly affect what you feel. You may begin thinking thoughts that did not originate in your head.

You may feel an invasion of your privacy, because on some level they feel what is going on in your life.

An Automatic Energy Exchange

You may feel tired after having been in a crowd of people. This is because you mix auras and also unknowingly exchange energy with other people. Just as a heat exchange occurs when you mix hot with cold, you exchange energy with other people.

This is one reason why older people or sick people enjoy youth so much. They automatically draw the energy of the younger or healthier person. This is an automatic process and is not something they consciously make happen.

If you are in a crowd, and there are some tired people in it or ones that may not feel well, they automatically draw your energy to them. Because crowds usually contain many tired, busy people, you sometimes feel drained fairly quickly.

Be Aware Of Your Boundary

If you are aware of the boundary of your own aura, you can pull it in by willing it to do so with your thoughts. Just as you reach out and pull a physical object toward you with your hand, reach out with your thoughts and pull your aura toward you. Feel the boundary of your aura change.

Creating A Bubble

Once you pull your aura in, place a clear bubble around it. This contains your aura within a specific boundary. All you have to do is take a second or two to visualize a bubble around your aura. Willing it to occur causes it to happen. This does not take place in your imagination. You actually create something with your thoughts.

The next time you are in a crowd, or among any group of people, consciously stop and take a couple of extra moments to pull your aura in and place a clear bubble around it.

You can do it once, or as many times as necessary to assure yourself that it is still there. Later when you are alone again, be aware of how you feel. Take a couple of seconds to determine if you are more comfortable and have more energy.

Family And Friends

Remember to use this tool when you are around family and friends. Maintain your bubble all the time because an automatic energy exchange takes place regardless of whom you are around. This does not make you have less feelings toward other people, but merely begins the sorting out process. You still feel, and the other person still feels.

The only difference is that you are able to focus in on the subject under discussion. You are no longer distracted by the feelings that are present in each aura. And, your communication actually becomes clearer, more open, and more direct. People become more comfortable because they are no longer mixing auras with you.

Keep Your Space Separate

Almost everyone has some type of emotional clutter surrounding them. Keep your space separate to help sort and organize your own feelings. This is a very basic beginning point for finding out who you are. If you react to situations through feelings that truly are not yours, you need to find this out. Defining your space allows you to do this.

REALISTIC EXPECTATIONS

One of the greatest pressures that you can put upon yourself is the perception of how you "should" be. You develop a list of rules for yourself that may be impossible to follow in practical terms. This list may be something that you have actually labeled, or, you may not even be aware that you have a list. The list that you use probably looks something like this:

I "should":

React to all situations calmly.

Never be angry, resentful, and/or bitter.

Always be understanding.

Be pleasant.

Speak patiently.

Have great relationships.

Be open and honest.

Be strong and supportive.

Always express love and peace.

Have clear direction in all situations.

The list can go on and on. When you consider what you

expect of yourself, the pressure of who you think you "should" be can be overwhelming. You chastise and criticize yourself whenever you act differently from the person that you think you "should" be. Your efforts are admirable but not realistic.

You Are Dual-Natured

In reality, you contain both positive *and* negative aspects. You are dual-natured. When you concentrate on overemphasizing the positive to compensate for the negative, you ignore a very important part of yourself.

Negative Aspects Are Important

Ignoring negative aspects do not make them go away. Instead, you only bury them deeper and deeper into your body, subconscious mind, and personal energy field, or aura.

Negative aspects are important:

They are an integral part of life.

They are excellent teachers.

When you are determined to ignore them, you may not realize how often they are the missing link in many of your dilemmas. Basic behavior patterns almost always contain both positive and negative components somewhere. When you ignore the negative, these patterns can be virtually impossible to identify.

Understanding this allows you to fill in the missing links, thus identifying specific behavior patterns. Once identified, you can make informed decisions on how, and if, you want to change these patterns. Learn to move through the discomfort of the negative by viewing it as a positive growth experience.

Acknowledging the existence of negative aspects gives you permission to recognize them as they occur. As you recognize them, you can label them. Then, you can study your life piece by piece, and diagnose it without judgment or criticism. This allows you to examine yourself as you are, and work with what is. It moves you through your illusions, and places you into reality.

Please recognize that your study of self-awareness is a slow, methodical route to a balanced change within. You will learn to appreciate your strengths *and* weaknesses. Thus, your growth potential will be reached. Because you make small, balanced, incremental adjustments within, you can easily accept the changes. In turn, this means that any changes you decide upon are effective and long-lasting.

Acknowledge Who You Are

Acknowledging who you are activates a process of self-healing as you stop hiding from yourself. All that you are is now out in the open. This openness allows you to accept yourself for who you are, instead of constantly criticizing yourself for who you are not.

You Are Where You Are Supposed to Be

You are where you are supposed to be with the tools, knowledge, and experience that you have. Realizing this allows you to change your list to one with more realistic expectations. It is much more realistic to say:

I *sometimes*:

React to situations calmly, but sometimes do not.

Am angry, resentful, and/or bitter, but sometimes am not.

Am understanding, but sometimes am not.

Am pleasant, but sometimes am not.

Speak patiently, but sometimes do not

Have great relationships, but sometimes do not.

Am open and honest, but sometimes am not.

Am strong and supportive, but sometimes need to be supported.

Express love and peace, but sometimes do not.

Have clear direction, but sometimes need guidance.

Be Gentle With Yourself

Changing your list helps you to be less strict with yourself. This develops a more gentle attitude toward who and what you are, and what you truly can expect from yourself with the tools, experience, and knowledge that you have. You develop more compassion and understanding for yourself.

You are not a "perfect" person or you would not be here. So, why are you expecting yourself to act like a "perfect" person? Striving toward growth is important, but do it in a way that is comfortable for you. Work within a realistic framework of expectations.

Everyone Is Learning

As you learn to be gentle with yourself, you develop true compassion and understanding for other people and their lives. Everyone is learning whether he/she consciously acknowledges it or not. There are many paths, and each one is made up of a variety of positive and negative experiences.

Everyone experiences whatever it is that he/she needs to lead that person deeper into his/her inner self, and deeper into God. No matter where anyone is in the evolutionary process, his/her path is just as difficult as yours, and just as important.

Respect everyone for the inner work that each is doing in the unique search for "self." Begin by respecting the work that you are doing and the path that you have chosen.

YOU HAVE THE ANSWERS

The challenges in your life did not just happen. They evolved through a series of actions that you set up over a course of time. On some level of awareness, you created them, so that you could learn and grow from them.

Because you created them, you have the knowledge to dismantle them. All you have to do is work backwards.

When you are in the middle of a challenge, it can be difficult to assess where you are, how you got there, and what you can do to get out of it. You may relate to the old saying, "You can't see the forest for the trees."

Recognize Specific Actions

You need a tool to help you recognize the specific actions that have created your challenges. Once you know what those actions are, **then** you can determine where you are, how you got there, and what you can do to get out of it.

Affirmations are very powerful and useful tools that bring specific answers to specific questions forward into your conscious mind. An affirmation is a statement in the present tense that defines a course of action, or a state of inner being. It is repeated many times by thinking, speaking, or writing it to bring new avenues of action into your conscious mind.

Using Affirmations

Both your positive and negative actions almost always combine together into patterns that create your challenges. Recognizing this, the affirmations that you choose provide answers that you can accept and utilize.

As an example, you may be experiencing a difficult relationship with your son. Your first thought might be that you try your hardest, and you do not understand why he acts the way that he does toward you.

Slow down and remember that your outer world is a reflection of you. Then ask the question, "What am I doing that is being reflected back to me by my son?." No matter how hard you think, you may not be able to come up with an answer.

You Already Know

An affirmation can bring that answer into your conscious mind, because on some level of awareness you already know. Start with a very basic affirmation that states the basic problem and your willingness to resolve it:

I am willing to release the conditions that create a negative relationship with my son.

To put the affirmation into motion, think of it throughout your day, speak it out loud if you wish, and most effectively, write it a minimum of ten times daily.

Because you are willing to release the conditions, they will surface up from your aura, up from your subconscious mind, and out of your physical body, where they have been buried. On their way out, they pass through your conscious mind. This identifies those conditions for you.

Positive And Negative Actions

Because both your positive and negative actions have combined into a pattern of behavior that has created your present challenge, expect both positive and negative actions to surface into your conscious mind.

For example, you may learn that you have tried to gain your son's love and approval by controlling and manipulating him. Wanting his love is a positive action. Your attempt to gain it through control and manipulation is a negative action. He resents your interference, and now he is rebelling.

You may learn that you are always criticizing and correcting him to "make him a better person." Wanting him to be a better person is a positive action. Criticizing and correcting to make him one is a negative action. He may not appreciate that, and expresses his disapproval through actions against you.

Or, perhaps you are still angry with him over specific childhood incidents. You *try* not to feel angry at him. That is a positive action. But, on some level, your anger still exists. That is a negative action. On some level, he feels and reacts to your anger.

Remember, there is no need to judge or criticize yourself when you identify these patterns of behavior. Realistically, you are where you are supposed to be with the tools, knowledge, and experience that you have. Be thankful that you are facing these parts of yourself so that you can learn from them, release them, and make specific changes.

Release The Conditions

Now that you are aware of the conditions that create the negative relationship, release them with the following affirmation:

I release the conditions that create a
negative relationship with my son.

You may want to release specific conditions, because they also create other negative relationships. Use one or more affirmations from the following subset:

I am willing to release my need to be
controlling and manipulative.

*I am willing to release my need to
criticize and correct.*

I am willing to release my need for anger.

Prepare For The New

As those aspects are released, prepare for a new relationship with your son. Change your affirmation to the following:

I am willing to accept a positive relationship with my son.

To enhance that positive relationship, use this subset of affirmations:

I allow my son to be who he wants to be.

*I allow myself to have relationships
centered around positive experiences.*

As your relationship improves, continue to change your affirmation to fit your present:

I accept a positive relationship with my son.

And, finally, change it one last time to pull you into a positive relationship with your son:

I now have a positive relationship with my son.

A Part Of The Process

Initially, this may look like a lot of work, and, in a way, it is. But, your relationship did not get to be the way it is overnight. It developed over many years. So, take the time to effect a long-lasting change instead of looking for a quick fix. Eventually, you will enjoy searching out the conditions and making the changes. It is all a part of the process:

You create a negative relationship.

You dismantle the negative relationship.

You create a positive relationship.

Affirmations Bridge Gaps

You may also need to design a series of affirmations to bridge the gap between what is, and what you want to be. For example, if your body is experiencing illness, you may choose the following affirmation:

I have a healthy body.

You may *want* to believe that your body is healthy, and you may *try* to believe that it is healthy, but this is not your reality. If your body is not experiencing health, it may be difficult to convince your conscious mind that it is. You may feel an internal struggle as you try to convince yourself that it is healthy.

At the end of this chapter you will find an example of a series of affirmations for a healthy body that you can use to help bridge the gap between your current and future reality.

A Five Step Process

When you are working hard to find an answer to a challenge that has you baffled, there is a process of designing affirmations that will maximize their effectiveness. It consists of the following five steps:

1. Find out what conditions are causing your present situation.
2. Release the old conditions.
3. Prepare yourself to accept the new conditions.
4. Accept the new conditions.
5. Affirm your new condition.

Utilizing these steps prepare the soil to accept the seed. If the soil is not properly cultivated, fertilized, and watered, the seed will have difficulty taking root. It is a very effective process, and the results are long-lasting.

Writing Affirmations

The most effective way to utilize affirmations is to write them. Get a notebook with lots of paper, and allow yourself

a few minutes every day to write the affirmation that you have chosen. If possible, set a specific time, such as first thing in the morning, or before you go to bed at night. Establish a routine that helps you follow through with your goals.

Writing affirmations may be a challenge in the beginning, but your results will encourage you. Experiment with different affirmations to see which ones feel right at the time. Finding affirmations that work for you becomes easier with practice. [Author's note: There are some short and simple affirmations in the appendices that you might enjoy using.]

Design Your Own

There is also a guideline for designing your own affirmations at the end of this chapter, followed by some examples. Start with the first one in the series, and write it a minimum of ten times daily. If you think about it during the day, repeat it silently or out loud.

When you feel comfortable that you have fully utilized the first affirmation, and have received answers that make sense to you, move on to the next affirmation in the series. In addition, work with the subset that you have developed. You will know when it is time to move on to the next one.

The more times that you write each affirmation, the faster you bring answers into your conscious mind. You may find that you do not have to use all five steps. You may be able to use two or three steps, depending on your challenge.

Affirmations Evolve

Eventually, your affirmations evolve on their own as you use the process. You do not have to think about the next step—it automatically occurs. One day, while writing your current affirmation, you may feel like changing it. You automatically flow with what is right for you—as a unique individual with a unique path into yourself.

Affirmations bring very immediate results. They teach you that you already have the answers. You, along with your Oversoul and God, can find any answer that you *need*. All that is necessary to get started is a few minutes a day, a piece of paper, a pen, and an open mind that allows you to try.

Guideline For Designing Affirmations

Using the following five step process, develop a series of affirmations that work for you. Start with the first affirmation, and when you are satisfied with the information that you have brought forward, *then* design your second one. When the second one has brought the answers forward that you need, *then* design your third, etc.

1. Find out what conditions are causing your present situation:

   I AM WILLING TO RELEASE THE CONDITIONS THAT CREATE...

   Make a list of those conditions as they come into your conscious mind.

2. Release the old conditions:

   I RELEASE THE CONDITIONS THAT CREATE...

   Develop a subset of affirmations.

3. Prepare yourself to accept the new conditions:

   I AM WILLING TO ACCEPT...

   Develop another subset of affirmations.

4. Accept the new conditions:

   I ACCEPT...

5. Affirm your new condition:

   I NOW AM/HAVE...

Affirmations For A Healthy Body

I AM WILLING TO RELEASE THE CONDITIONS THAT CREATE *ILLNESS*.

This affirmation brings the conditions that create illness into your conscious mind. Those conditions might be:

It gives me extra attention from family and friends.

It gives me a chance to talk about me.

It teaches me how to take care of my body through negative learning.

(Specific thought and behavior patterns that create my specific illness).

I RELEASE THE CONDITIONS THAT CREATE *ILLNESS*.

You may need a subset of affirmations:

I release the need for negative attention.

I release the need to learn about my body in a negative way.

I release the need for (specific thought and behavior patterns that create my specific illness).

I AM WILLING TO ACCEPT *A HEALTHY BODY*.

You may need another subset of affirmations:

I am willing to accept positive attention.

I am willing to learn about my body in a positive way.

I am willing to change (specific thought and behavior patterns that create my specific illness).

I ACCEPT *A HEALTHY BODY*.

I NOW HAVE *A HEALTHY BODY*.

Affirmations For Prosperity

I AM WILLING TO RELEASE THE CONDITIONS THAT CREATE *LACK*.

This affirmation brings the conditions that create lack into your conscious mind. Those conditions might be:

My mother told me I would never amount to much.

Other people are prosperous, but it won't happen to me.

I am not worthy of prosperity.

I do not deserve prosperity.

I RELEASE THE CONDITIONS THAT CREATE *LACK*.

Your subset of affirmations becomes:

I forgive my mother for her words.

I forgive myself for believing them.

I am a worthwhile and deserving person.

I AM WILLING TO ACCEPT *PROSPERITY*.

Your next subset of affirmations becomes:

I am worthy of prosperity.

I deserve prosperity.

I ACCEPT *PROSPERITY*.

I NOW AM *PROSPEROUS*.

Affirmations For Positive Relationships

I AM WILLING TO RELEASE THE CONDITIONS THAT CREATE *NEGATIVE RELATIONSHIPS*.

This affirmation brings the conditions that create negative relationships into your conscious mind. Those conditions might be:

I am controlling and manipulative.

I am complaining and criticizing.

I hold inner hostility toward people in my life.

I RELEASE THE CONDITIONS THAT CREATE *NEGATIVE RELATIONSHIPS*.

Your subset of affirmations becomes:

I am willing to release my need to be controlling and manipulative.

I am willing to release my need to complain and criticize.

I am willing to release my need to be hostile.

I AM WILLING TO ACCEPT *POSITIVE RELATION-SHIPS*.

Your next subset of affirmations becomes:

I allow everyone to be who each wants to be.

I allow myself to have relationships centered around positive experiences.

I ACCEPT *POSITIVE RELATIONSHIPS*.

I NOW HAVE *POSITIVE RELATIONSHIPS*.

INTO THE SILENCE

Meditation is the most versatile and flexible tool that you can take with you in search of yourself. Easy to use, it quickly becomes very personal, and allows you to touch into continually deeper levels of inner awareness. The process of going within automatically changes you and your reactions to your inner and outer worlds.

Meditation is a process that must be used in order to understand it. It produces feelings inside of yourself that connect you to who and what you are.

Meditation takes you beyond words and puts you in touch with the level of feeling. Because you are so accustomed to identifying with words instead of with feelings, the process of meditation appears very elusive. It is actually a simple activity that only through definition has become complex.

The process of meditation allows you the opportunity to slow down long enough to refocus your attention from your outer to inner world. It pulls your concentration into one focal point and directs it inward. It allows you to sink deeper and deeper into your center, melding your conscious, subconscious, and superconscious minds with your Oversoul and God.

Concentration

Almost everyone has the skill of concentration. It develops as you go through life. It takes concentration to play a game of basketball, knit an afghan, study for a test, or work at a computer. Somewhere in your life, you are already applying the skill of concentration. To meditate, all you have to do is redirect your concentration from your outer to inner world.

Inner Pressures

There are many inner pressures that prevent you from meditating before you even begin. For example, sometimes even saying the word "meditation" can make you feel awkward. Telling your family that you need time alone to meditate may make you feel uncomfortable. Your involve-

ment in a new activity may be hard for them to accept.

If they give you a difficult time, remember, this is their way of coping with something new in their lives. They feel uncomfortable, so they are trying to make you feel uncomfortable, too. If you give up your new activity, they will not have to deal with it.

Respect yourself enough to find time to meditate. Eventually, your family will respect your request for time alone and privacy.

Finding A Time

Find a time during the day or evening that is comfortable for you. Do your best to meditate on a regular schedule. Just as your stomach prepares itself to eat around your regular mealtimes, your body and mind automatically prepare themselves as your meditation time approaches. Set a time limit that works for you, establishes a routine, and fits into your daily schedule.

Right now, you may feel enthused and decide to meditate thirty minutes a day. You have no trouble finding the time to meditate on the first and second day. On the third day, something happens to interrupt your schedule, and you never get to it. By the fourth day, you think that you "should," but that is as far as you get.

By now, your original enthusiasm is gone, and either you have to rekindle it or you never start again. Your total experience with meditation was sixty minutes. This means that your original enthusiasm could be converted to equal sixty minutes.

Spending Your Enthusiasm

Rather than spend those sixty minutes of original enthusiasm quickly in two days, a more productive way would be to meditate for twelve days at five minutes per day. Your original enthusiasm remains the same, but you can usually fit five minutes into your schedule. A five minute routine is easier to maintain. Leave yourself wanting more rather than sabotaging your good intentions right from the start.

Give yourself a couple of weeks to decide if meditation is something that you want to pursue. If it is, then increase your time to ten minutes a day. After a few more weeks, and you are still maintaining your meditation time, then increase it to fifteen minutes.

Fifteen minutes a day is a good amount of time to devote to meditation once you have an established routine. As time goes by, you may find your time automatically increasing. You may sit to meditate for fifteen minutes, and the next thing you know, twenty minutes have passed, or thirty. Never increase your time because you think you "should." Only increase it when you genuinely want to.

Sitting Quietly

Another inner pressure may be your inability to sit quietly. Sitting quietly can be more difficult than it sounds. For example, it is not always easy to sit quietly when you are involved in an active lifestyle. There are so many activities to catch your attention, sitting quietly is not usually top priority.

The only experience you may have with sitting quietly is as a disciplinary action from your parents. When you sit to meditate, the child within you wants to squirm around. On some level, you still react to your past experiences.

Your lifestyle and past experiences often prevent you from sitting quietly, and the collective unconscious does not give you much encouragement. Western society is very material-oriented and expects you to produce something. It expects you to be able to justify your time to the outer world. You can count the number of pages read in a book or miles driven in a car. But what have you produced when you sit quietly? Your training teaches you to produce, and you feel strange when you are not.

Sitting quietly is a skill that must be developed and integrated into your lifestyle. There are some suggestions in the appendices to help if this is difficult for you.

The Primary Purpose Of Meditation

The primary purpose of meditation is to establish a direct link to your Oversoul and God by opening the doors between your conscious, subconscious, and superconscious minds. These doors are made of silence. Silence is the level of feeling. As these doors open, you begin to know by knowing.

Your conscious mind contains your present.

Your subconscious mind contains your memories, moment by moment, lifetime by lifetime.

Your superconscious mind provides the direct link to your Oversoul and God.

During meditation, allow yourself to sink continually deeper into silence, the level of feeling. Feel yourself expand into your center and beyond your physical body. As you alter your conscious state, there is a feeling of movement. This is the natural rhythm of the universe that expands and contracts.

Everything exists and nothing exists simultaneously within the silence. It is here that you connect with your Oversoul and God through the level of feeling. Your Oversoul gently pushes whatever you need to know through the doors of silence and into your conscious mind.

Connecting with your Oversoul can occur within seconds, or, it can take a long time. It depends upon your ability to sit quietly so that you can feel. You may be getting information now from your Oversoul without even being aware of it because you are unaccustomed to communicating through feeling. Feelings occur first, and then the words are attached to explain those feelings. The process must be slowed down and defined to repeat it at will.

Three Keys To Successful Meditation

There are three keys to successful meditation:

Start from where you are—

If sitting quietly for five minutes is difficult, then practice just sitting.

Move into the next steps when you feel comfortable doing so.

Do not expect too much—

This only puts pressure on you that you do not need.

Go with what you get—

There is always a reason for whatever is passing before you.

As an example, if you have wandering thoughts that will not stop, perhaps they are providing you with information that you previously overlooked—pay attention to them.

Breathing Correctly

Your breath is an important part of the process of meditation. Focusing your attention on your breath pulls your attention further inward. Because of this, it is important that you breathe correctly. As strange as it sounds, not everyone knows how to breathe just because they are getting air into their lungs.

Women are especially likely to breathe incorrectly. They often learn at an early age to hold their stomachs in so that they look thinner and more attractive. As a result, they often tend to breathe with their upper chest rather than utilizing the full capacity of their lungs.

To determine if you are breathing correctly, lay your hand on your stomach. When you inhale, your stomach will inflate. When you exhale, your stomach will deflate. If you are not breathing in this manner, practice filling your lungs from the bottom up, while lying down. Then practice breathing while sitting, standing, walking, etc. It is important to breathe correctly when you begin your practice of meditation.

When you have learned to sit quietly, and to breathe correctly, then experiment with the following guideline:

Guideline for Meditation

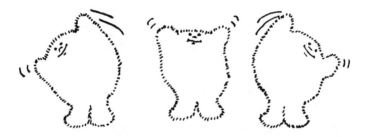

Gently bend and stretch to release any tension in your body.

Sitting in a comfortable chair, keep your feet flat on the floor, or,

> Sit in a variation of the yoga lotus position, or,

> Lie down, keeping your legs stretched out straight and untangled, being careful not to fall asleep (!).

Position your hands palm up in a receptive position.

Keep your spine straight—

> This allows for optimum energy flow through the primary energy centers that are aligned along it.

Close your eyes.

Visualize where the center of your being is located—

Notice that it is aligned along your spine.

Pull your attention in from your outer world by willing all of your thoughts into your center.

Stop and feel how safe it is to be in your center.

Focus your attention on your third eye area—

Do this by placing a finger on your forehead between your eyebrows and look at it from the inside, keeping your eyes closed.

Breathe in from the top of your head to the base of your spine.

Breathe out from the base of your spine through the top of your head.

Feel your breath pull your concentration further inward.

Watch your breath as it goes up and down, in and out—

Give it weight, color, and consistency.

Notice that your breath creates a vacuum that pulls you deeper into your center.

Eventually, as soon as you start the breathing process, your breath will automatically pull you into your center.

Allow your breathing to return to normal.

Notice how calm and quiet you feel.

(Should you wish to do so, it is at this time that you will do your meditative work).

Remember the feeling so that you can touch into it throughout the day.

Open your eyes.

Many Levels Of Awareness

There are many levels of awareness in meditation, and as you experiment, you will find them. The first level contains your wandering thoughts. It is normal for your thoughts to wander. When they do, simply acknowledge that they are wandering, and release them up to your Oversoul. Go back to your breathing.

The deepest level is silence. Because this is the level of feeling, words are not necessary. In fact, there are no words that can adequately express what occurs in silence. It is something that you must experience to understand. At this point, suffice it to say that when you touch into silence, you have immediate understanding of whatever it is that you feel. As you go further into the process of meditation, you will understand.

Touching into silence for even a few seconds is progress. Those few seconds provide the trail to follow deeper within. In the middle are many levels of awareness. This is where you do your meditative work.

Working From Your Center

Your center provides a safe place from which to work, and it is here that you observe and evaluate yourself. It is a place where you are without judgment or self-criticism.

In your center, you can safely examine whatever you are outwardly expressing. You can make decisions about which behavior patterns you want to keep and which ones you are ready to discard. From here, you release anything that you no longer need up to your Oversoul. You can make any decision that you want while you are in your center.

Objectively Observing

When you meditate, assume the role of an objective observer. This allows you to sort and file the information that you collect from your experiences. To gather your data, ask the following questions as you review the experiences that pass before your inner eye:

How did I act and react?

How did other people act and react?

What did I learn?

What remains to be learned?

What will I do the next time I have the same type of experience?

What was my cumulative learning from the experience?

Remember, you are objectively observing, i.e., you are not criticizing or judging. You are only evaluating what exists in order to accurately interpret the data. *Then*, make a conscious decision about any behavior patterns that you wish to change.

As you evaluate, release all of your observations up to your Oversoul. Check every corner of yourself to see what emotions are surfacing. Instead of denying any negative emotions that you find, experience them. Express to your Oversoul whatever it is that you feel.

Acknowledge All Emotion

Never suppress, ignore, or deny any emotion. You cannot release it unless you recognize that it exists. As long as you stay in your center, you are safe. You are accustomed to suppressing your negative emotions, because in the past it was too easy to let them control you.

From your center, as an objective observer who studies the subject, watch any part of you that contains negative emotion. Observe that it is a part of you, but it is not you. Remember, it can teach you if you let it.

Allow it to express its feelings as you watch from your center. When it is finished, pass it out of you by releasing it up to your Oversoul.

Learn To Know By Knowing

Return any information that surfaces into your conscious mind during meditation without explanation to your Oversoul. Your goal is to know by knowing. If you retain unexplained information, you tie yourself to a level of guessing. You want to pass into deeper levels of awareness so that you have an instant explanation for any information that you receive.

Meditation Suggestions

The following examples are what you can do while meditating:

Ask for guidance.

Clean out painful experiences.

Clean out pleasant experiences to make room for more.

Heal your mental, emotional, physical, and spiritual bodies.

Ask that healing be sent to all life forms in accordance with their needs and the wishes of their Oversouls.

Explore ideas.

Relax.

Review and release your daily life so that you do not build a storehouse of experiences you no longer need.

Allow past lifetimes to surface when it is appropriate, and when they have specific meaning to you.

Enter into silence, the level of feeling.

Be selective of how you spend your meditation time. Decide what is important for you to know. Ask for guidance from your Oversoul—and pursue that course of action.

Meditation Experiences Are Unique

Each person has different experiences during meditation. All experiences are equal in importance. No one has a

"better" experience than someone else. While meditating you may experience color, lights, sound, taste, smell, or pictures. Someone else may not. This does not mean that your experiences are better. It only means that each person is a unique individual on his/her own unique path to God.

Your goal is to move through the color, lights, sounds, tastes, smells, and pictures into continually deeper levels of awareness, into silence. This is the level of feeling that allows you to know by knowing by melding with your Oversoul and God. How you do that is very personal, and it is up to you and your Oversoul to determine how you will accomplish it.

Incorporating Your Learning

Your learning from your meditations automatically incorporates itself into your daily living. For example, if you experience calmness during meditation, stop and touch into it throughout the day. No matter how hectic the pace of your outer world, pull yourself into your center and survive that pace without having it pull you apart. Walk through your outer turmoil knowing that it only exists for you to learn about you.

Your learning extends into other areas of your outer world as well, such as:

Your concentration improves in every area of your life.

You observe your daily actions with less criticism and judgment—

This allows you to be more gentle with yourself.

This allows you to become more acceptable to yourself.

You understand instead of criticize and judge the actions of other people.

You release your experiences to your Oversoul as they occur, no longer carrying unnecessary vibratory imprints with you.

Your aura becomes cleaner and clearer.

You become more relaxed.

Your body looks younger.

Your body functions more efficiently.

You stop reacting to your present through your past experiences.

Your ability to communicate with your outer world improves.

You acknowledge and understand inner communication as it occurs.

Meditation also teaches you to quiet your thinking mind. A quiet mind means a clear mind. A clear mind is much more perceptive and accurate in its observations and evaluations.

Understanding The Process

The more you work with the process of meditation, the more you understand what meditation is. Meditation produces feelings that no one can ever adequately explain with words. You must experience it to understand the feelings that it produces. Then, you can go back and say, "I know what you are talking about." The knowledge becomes yours because you have experienced it and you have learned through direct awareness.

WHAT IS GOD?

All that is comes out of God. You are a part of God that determines the totality of God. You are a microcosm of the macrocosm. Your very basic building blocks come out of God.

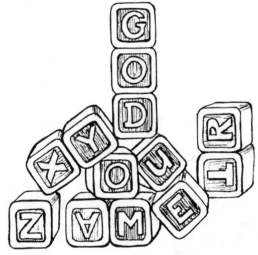

For comparison, think about all the shapes that water can take:

Water is liquid—

Yet, it can also become ice, steam, or gas depending upon the rate of vibration of its atoms and molecules.

The substances look entirely different to the naked eye.

Yet, they all clearly originate from the same basic building blocks.

In the same way, you, your Oversoul, and God are all neutral energy.

God Is Neutral Energy

God is neutral energy that is in the process of explaining itself by experiencing itself. Out of God was birthed all that is seen and all that is not seen. All that God provides acknowledges the existence of God.

God is in a continual process of experiencing God. God is rearranging God to answer the questions:

What am I?

What functions can I perform?

What shapes can I take?

What colors am I?

How deep am I?

How high am I?

What do I feel?

How many ways can I feel it?

Everything Is An Expression of God

As you practice the process of meditation you automatically understand that everything is an expression of God. Through direct awareness, you feel a connection with all that is. That connection allows you to feel a oneness with the earth, the sky, and the sea; with plants and trees; with animals; and with other people.

You feel that oneness pulling you into itself. And, you understand what that oneness is. Direct awareness is teaching you about God. You feel "I am a part of God; I am a part of all that is."

As an example, the ocean may be used as an analogy to God. You are not the ocean (God), but you are a wave upon the ocean. You are very connected to it, with the potential to experience it by blending with it. Understanding the ocean begins by analyzing one drop of water. In the same way, understanding the microcosm, you, deepens your understanding of the macrocosm, God.

The Word "God"

Sometimes the word "God" makes people feel uncomfortable. Often the reason is because "the name of God" has been used to justify many negative actions, such as war and violence. The vibrations from those actions have gone out into the collective unconscious and stuck to the word "God."

When people hear the word "God," they may feel the injustices that have been associated with its use. They may be reacting to the actions surrounding the word, rather than to the word itself. "God" is actually a very pure and clear word that has lost some of its clarity through its use.

You Are A Story

As a part of God, you are a unique set of experiences that continues to answer the question, "What is God?". You are a story waiting to be told, and you have the ability to tell your own story.

It would be very boring if you sat down to read a novel whose first page said, "The man was murdered." and whose second page said, "The butler did it. The end." The reasons you read the novel are for entertainment, to learn strategy, and to challenge your mind. You like putting together the clues and matching your mental abilities against the author's. You want to know all about the beginning, the middle, and the resolution. Each part of the novel is equally important.

The same is true of your life. It contains many chapters with beginnings, middles, and resolutions. Some chapters are still in progress and are unresolved. You may be avoiding the difficult chapters by looking the other way and hoping they resolve themselves. Just as you read a novel for intrigue, challenge, and entertainment, you set up your own personal story in the same way, for the same reasons.

Are You Choosing Pain And Suffering?

Why would anyone choose to put pain, suffering, misery, or discomfort into their lives? Why would actors or actresses choose any role but a happy one? Why would they want to make people sad, or scare them? Why would they want to portray someone with mental or physical handicaps?

The answer for them is the same as it is for you: learning, growth, and experience. They want to see how they feel, act, and react, and they want to see how other people feel, act, and react.

You are here to experience, and experience means learning and growth. Becoming comfortable in a pattern of behavior that you no longer need can be easy, because moving out of it means moving into the unknown. The unknown can be very scary, even if it is a change for the better.

Pain, suffering, misery, and discomfort often move you when nothing else will. When you are uncomfortable enough, you opt to change something. It could be a very minor, or a very major change, but it always denotes learning and growth.

There are perks to pain, suffering, misery, and discomfort that you may not consciously recognize. For instance, they often provide the avenue for extra attention, sympathy, caring, and tenderness that you might not otherwise receive, or perhaps not even feel that you deserve. Stop and identify the benefits that your pain brings you.

Giving Your Power Away

Giving your power away by letting someone else tell you how and what you are, satisfies your instant curiosity. But, after that is gone, you have an empty feeling because you did not have the opportunity, or the satisfaction, or the thrill, of finding the knowledge that is deep within you.

Allowing other people to give you answers that you are capable of finding, provides a buffer that keeps you from becoming too involved with yourself. It keeps discomfort at a distance. Once it is close, you have to feel it and deal with it, and you may not be ready to do that yet.

Let other people act as a catalyst to help direct you, but do as much as you can on your own. When it is necessary, ask for only enough information to give you a boost so that you can do some more.

If you do decide to give your power away, then at least do so in conscious awareness. Recognize and label what you are doing. When you are ready, take back your power. Use it to delve into yourself and read your own story.

There Are No Failures

Your life does have meaning within itself, and in relationship to the overall purpose of human drama. There are no failures, only circumstances that show you your strengths and weaknesses. Acknowledge these circumstances for what they are: tools that you have developed for yourself. Recognize that others have had these same experiences before you. More will have them after you have passed through them. You are never alone in your learning.

Your Experiences Come From God

All of your experiences come from God. You can choose to understand or not understand what is happening to you. But, it will happen anyway. Asking questions and objectively evaluating yourself from every perspective allows you to flow with your experiences.

You may still have the same experiences, but you understand and learn from them. You agree to them, knowing that you will be stronger and wiser when they are completed. You will not fight them, but accept them. This allows you to move with and through them, and on into the next one, knowing that each experience continues to explain you to you, and in turn, God to God.

Explore Who You Are

In order to understand the experiences that have made you who and what you are, be willing to explore who you are. Walk through your fears of the unknown, realizing that you are afraid, but that you are willing to try. Appreciate every experience, slowing down long enough to give every moment equal meaning and importance.

Meditation gives you the opportunity to develop a safe, quiet place to make accurate evaluations about who and what you are; a place to evaluate your strengths, your weaknesses, and your potential. A place where you can learn about you.

The more you learn about yourself, the more you appreciate yourself. You realize that you are the most fascinating and interesting person that you know.

The more that you appreciate yourself, the deeper you are able to go during meditation. The deeper you go, the more you learn about God; the more you learn about God, the more you learn about yourself.

The circle will perpetuate itself if you let it:

You learn about yourself, you learn about God, You learn about God, You learn about yourself, You understand the microcosm, you understand the macrocosm, You understand the microcosm. You understand the macrocosm.

Your ability to access knowledge is only limited by your willingness to move.

WHAT ARE YOU?

During meditation you are aware that you are moving into places where your physical body cannot go. You understand that there is more to you than the physical body. You, as a microcosm of the macrocosm, are individualized neutral energy.

As energy you do not have arms and hands, or legs and feet. If you could look directly into the sun on a bright day, what you would see looks very similar to what you actually look like. Ask to be shown what you look like during meditation.

Through inner awareness, you understand that you *have* a physical body, but you are *not* your body. Your physical body came from the bodies of your biological parents. Their bodies provided the avenue for you to enter into this dimension. Their bodies are the parents of your *body*, but they are not *your* parents.

The beings whom you call "Mom" and "Dad" have chosen to experience this lifetime with you. They may or may not be your biological parents in future lifetimes. Regardless, the learning that they give you in this lifetime is important.

Oversouls

The neutral energy that is called God is the equivalent of your grandmother/grandfather. Out of God came smaller portions of neutral energy called Oversouls. Oversouls also look similar to the sun on a bright day, but are much larger than you. Every person has an Oversoul. The equivalent of a mother/father, it is where *you* came from. It is *your* parent. Your Oversoul remains the same lifetime after lifetime.

GOD
Grandmother/Grandfather

Oversoul
Mother/Father

You
and
others

Your Oversoul also provides the intermediary link between God, a very vast energy, and you, a small portion of that vast energy. Your Oversoul is a type of buffer between you and God. For example, you could not plug your kitchen toaster directly into an electric generator at a dam. The wattage from the electric generator would be too powerful, and would burn out the toaster.

Instead, you plug your toaster into a smaller wattage through an electrical outlet in your home. If you compare yourself to the toaster and the electric generator to God, you understand why you need the electrical outlet, or, your Oversoul.

Everything has an Oversoul for effective communication with God. There are Oversouls for the mineral kingdom, the plant kingdom, and the animal kingdom, as well as humankind. There are many Oversouls for each group. For example, one Oversoul is the parent of many men and women.

Each Individual Is Important

Each individual is important to its Oversoul. Personal identity is not lost, but enhanced. Each individual consists of unique experiences that contribute to the whole. Put another way, it is similar to the cells and organs in your body. Each cell and group of organs in your body has a special role. Your heart contributes something that your liver does not, and vice versa. Your body does not need two hearts or two livers, but one of each to function efficiently.

Each individual that belongs to the same Oversoul contributes his/her own unique experiences. For example, occupations, family and social relationships, and emotional experiences vary. Each individual contributes something that the others do not. As your Oversoul gathers your experiences and understanding, it passes them on to God. In this way, God continues to explain God by experiencing God.

God Needs To Experience God

You may wonder why God needs to experience God to explain God. Perhaps you can relate to the following analogy. You may love to swim. Sitting at home, in your easy chair, you know a lot about swimming. You know how the water feels, how your body feels, and how you feel.

You can think about swimming all you want, but it is not quite the same as actually swimming. If it were, you would never leave your easy chair. Swimming produces feelings that must be experienced. Only when you have experienced swimming can you adequately explain what it is. In the same way, God needs to experience God to explain God.

Your Oversoul Knows Your Life

Your Oversoul knows the entire picture of your life, from the beginning to the end. You are usually only aware of a portion of your life. This allows you to focus on the present moment in order to learn as you go. If you knew the outcome of your experiences, you would discount the importance of the present moment.

Making A Contract

Between lives, you make a contract with yourself and your Oversoul. This contract decides the general direction that your life will take in order to provide the learning that you need to fulfill your commitments to yourself, your

Oversoul, and God. You are then born into those circumstances that allow you to complete that contract if you choose to complete it.

You always have free will to change your mind, but sooner or later, you will have to come back to finish what you started. It is in your best interest to take a deep breath and move into your life.

You enter into this world without conscious knowledge of this contract. If you knew your life experiences in advance, you might be overwhelmed. However, as you grow, you develop the necessary skills to meet the challenges that come your way.

You may wonder why you would have agreed to your current challenges. You sign up for your life experiences in the same way that you sign up for any school. For example, in high school, you decide on a career as an engineer. At this time, you plan your college program. Once you are actually in college, you may find that some courses are more difficult than you had anticipated. Yet, you still know that you need them in order to become an engineer. In the same way, there are going to be some difficult moments in your life, but what you learn from them prepares you for your future.

You Are Connected By A Channel

There is a clear, elasticized channel that connects you to your Oversoul. On some level of awareness, you may already be communicating with your Oversoul, depending upon the contract that you agreed to before you were born. You can open this channel through meditation and prayer, and develop conscious communication with your Oversoul.

Conscious Communication

The primary way that you now consciously communicate with your Oversoul is through physical death. You may have heard stories of people going through purgatory when they die. What they are actually doing is relaying their lifetime of experiences to their Oversoul so that together they can evaluate their life: what they learned and what remains to be learned. At this time, they start formulating the contract for their next lifetime.

Sometimes, you may even compile many lifetimes before you share them with your Oversoul. This means that you and your body are full of vibrations from past experiences that you no longer need.

You can consciously share your experiences with your Oversoul now. Rather than accumulate them for one or more lifetimes, you can release the vibrations of your experiences as they occur. As you do so, you become cleaner, lighter, and more flexible. This allows your mental, emotional, physical, and spiritual bodies to function more effectively because they are no longer bogged down with weight that they no longer need.

Conscious communication with your Oversoul means assuming more responsibility for your personal development. This gives you the chance to modify the contract that you agreed to many years ago, before you were born.

Instead of waiting until after-the-fact to share your life with your Oversoul, you can share it now. As an active participant, state the reasons why your life should or should not follow a particular course of action. Become an active partner in your own growth.

Prepare Your Next Life

Prepare your next life while you are here. Tell your Oversoul what you do and do not want, as long as you let it make the final decision. Fine tuning a situation while you are actually involved in it is much easier than waiting until it is over.

For example, relate back to planning four years of college. Once those four years of college are over, it is easy to forget exactly how difficult those four years were. Those years are past, and your attention is now on other experiences. But, if you knew that you would be attending college again in another twenty years, it would be possible to take careful notes about what to look for the next time around. You can do the same when it comes to your life. You might not get everything that you want, but with some effort, you can come a little closer.

Use The Lines Of Communication

Although your Oversoul establishes an effective link between you and God, you can also share your life directly with God. There is a hierarchy, but you may use it however you like. As a comparison, you may sometimes wish to talk to your grandparents as well as, or instead of, your parents. The lines of communication are always open.

Your Oversoul helps you learn, and is always available. It is your partner as well as your parent. Ask it to guide you into your potential in order to continue experiencing all that is important to your individual growth. Allow it to direct you into even deeper levels of inner awareness.

Experiment And Question

The concept of Oversouls is touched upon in various esoteric writings. Determine for yourself if the concept is valid. Experiment with the ideas presented, and decide if they make sense. Gather the data, and evaluate it for yourself. Ask what an Oversoul looks and feels like during meditation. And remember—keep an open mind and be willing to try.

INNER COMMUNICATIONS

Before you learn how to communicate with your inner world, it is important to first understand how you communicate with your outer world.

Psychic Energy

Definition:

Psychic energy is your own personal energy. It flows back and forth and is horizontal. It is not good or bad, it just is.

Psychic energy moves the physical body and helps with communication in the outer world. For example, psychic energy is used to talk, walk, listen, digest food, etc. As psychic energy is depleted, the amount available to the physical body diminishes.

When you talk, you feel energy flow out of your mouth. You feel it flow horizontally. When you listen, you feel the horizontal energy of the other person hit your ears. Sometimes, on some level, you may almost feel invaded when people talk to you. You feel the harshness of the energy that they send toward you.

Mixing Auras

Because psychic energy moves back and forth, it passes through your aura and the vibratory imprints of your accumulated past experiences. When you talk to someone he/she feels more than your words. On some level of awareness he/she also feels the feelings of your past experiences.

Passing through your aura, your words pick up the feelings of your past experiences. Then, as this energy moves into another person's aura, it picks up the feelings of his/her accumulated past experiences. The energy that eventually hits his/her ears is loaded up with all of these feelings. This mixes auras and creates discomfort on some level of awareness.

Feel The Energy

Stop and feel the energy that people use when they communicate. Feel the horizontal flow of the energy as it moves back and forth. Feel the energy of your own words as you talk.

Universal Energy

Your physical body needs your psychic energy to function. Maximize the amount of psychic energy available to it by working with universal energy.

Definition:

Universal energy is energy that is available to everyone. It flows up and down and is vertical.

Universal energy allows you to communicate with your Oversoul. You are connected through the top of your head to your Oversoul by a clear, elasticized channel. Using universal energy, communication flows vertically between you and your Oversoul through this channel.

Because universal energy flows through this channel, it passes through a different area of your aura. This creates a cleaner, clearer energy.

Your Breathing Work Prepares The Channel

The breathing work in meditation prepares you to use universal energy. It starts your energy moving up and down.

With your breath, continue to open and expand the channel. As you exhale, send it all the way up the channel into your Oversoul. As you inhale, bring your breath back down the channel to the base of your spine.

If you see or feel any dark, accumulated debris, use your breath as a scrub brush to clean it out. As you move your breath up and down, pass the loosened debris on up the channel to your Oversoul.

Feeling The Channel

Working with your breath also deepens your level of inner awareness. As an example, feel the difference in the

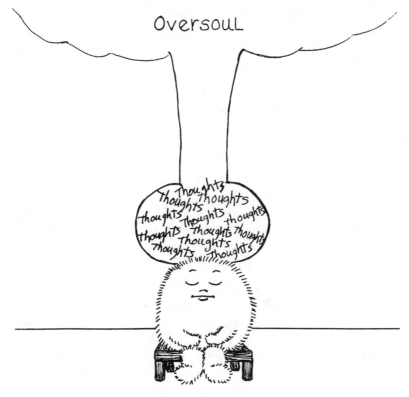

Oversoul

substances that your breath passes through. Starting at the base of your spine, exhale up and out of your body. Feel your breath pass through the space that contains your physical body. As your breath passes out the top of your head, feel the space that sits directly on top of your head. This space contains your thoughts.

It feels different than the space that holds your physical body. The next space that you pass into is the channel that connects you to your Oversoul. It also has a specific feeling.

It feels like "empty space" when compared to the space that holds your thoughts. While your breath is in the channel, will yourself outside the channel for a moment. Feel the difference between being inside and outside the channel.

Moving Into The Channel

To communicate with your Oversoul, push through your physical body, out the top of your head, through your own thoughts, and into the channel. When you push up high enough, you can communicate with your Oversoul.

In the beginning, it may be difficult to know that anything is happening. Your communications may be so subtle that you are not able to separate them from your own thoughts and feelings. That is why it is important to push up above the space that contains your own thoughts.

If you do not, then you may have difficulty distinguishing your own thoughts and feelings from the feelings of your Oversoul. Your reasoning mind tries to talk you out of whatever it is that you feel. The more you use the channel, the more perceptive you are to the communications that flow down it.

More Accurate Observations

Moving your energy up and down, instead of back and forth, enables you to examine your life with greater accuracy. No longer looking horizontally through your accumulated vibratory imprints, you look at it from above, as an objective observer. This means you make more accurate observations.

Activating The Process

As you objectively observe, pass your data up the channel to your Oversoul. Ask your Oversoul to evaluate it and return the conclusions to you. Continue to move the energy up and down, even if you are unsure that anything is happening. Using the process activates the process. Eventually, you understand it through direct awareness. Then you can say, "I know by knowing; now I understand what I was reading about".

Your data goes up the channel, and the evaluations come back down. Each time you use the channel, you push your energy up. As you utilize the channel, you find that you pass through your own conclusions first. With practice, you feel the differences between your own conclusions and those of your Oversoul.

Feeling The Conclusions

You feel your own conclusions in the space above your head. You feel the conclusions of your Oversoul in the area of "empty space" above your thoughts. Sometimes it is difficult to push up high enough to access the conclusions of your Oversoul. You like your own so well that it is easy to stop with them. Move through them, going up higher into the channel.

"Hunches"

You may already be using universal energy and communicating with your Oversoul without being aware of it. At some time during your life you have probably followed a "hunch" with successful results. Usually, you label these hunches "intuition".

You may have said, "I had a *feeling* to do thus and so, and I'm glad I did". Sometimes, you have a *feeling* to do something, but you let your reasoning mind talk you out of it. Then, after-the-fact, you tell yourself that you "should" have done thus and so because you had a *feeling* that told you to.

Those *feelings* are communications from your Oversoul, but, without awareness of the process, you cannot repeat the experience at will. You have to passively wait for another "hunch".

You are now slowing down the process, defining it, and labeling it so that you can use it at will. Using the process allows you to actively go within and get a "hunch" whenever you need one. Using the process refines it so that your "hunches" become more accurate.

Communicating With Other People

Using universal energy to communicate with other people is clean and efficient. Feel your words pass up the channel

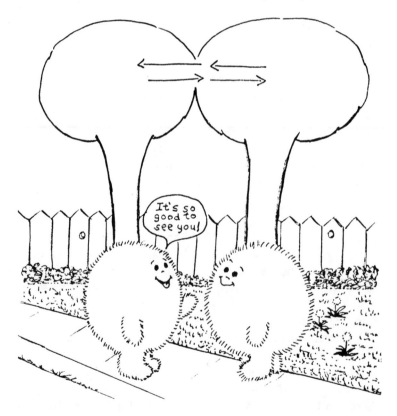

to your Oversoul whenever you speak to someone. Observe that your energy flows vertically rather than horizontally.

Ask your Oversoul to pass your words on to the other person's Oversoul, down his/her channel, and through the top of his/her head. Visualize the process happening. This keeps your words clean and their meaning clear.

Whenever you want to talk to someone, silently speak first through your Oversoul, even if it is only to say hello. This catches the person's attention on another level, and redirects their concentration towards you. It prepares that person for your conversation before it occurs.

Before talking to someone, always silently speak through your Oversoul first. Another individual does not have to be physically present for you to talk to him/her. On some level of awareness the person receives your message, thus preparing him/her for your conversation.

Because he/she receives your message on another level, fewer spoken words are necessary. You might not even have to say much at all. The other person may address your concerns or answer your questions before you speak.

Ask Your Oversoul To Help

Whenever anyone speaks to you, visualize a giant hand inside of your head scooping the words up the channel to your Oversoul. Ask your Oversoul to clean up the words so that you understand the feeling behind them.

When you read, feel the written words go up the channel. Ask your Oversoul to explain the material as it directly relates to you. Whenever you want to remember something, pass that information up the channel, and ask your Oversoul to remember it for you.

Pass all of your observations up the channel to your Oversoul. If there is anything that you need to know, ask your Oversoul to point it out to you.

Although in the beginning the process may feel cumbersome and awkward, it eventually will become spontaneous. In comparison, when you were a child learning to eat, using a knife, fork, and spoon felt very cumbersome and awkward. It took concentration and practice to use those tools and get the food into your mouth, not all over your face. As an adult, you use those same utensils effortlessly. By the same token, as you practice the tools of communication just outlined, the more natural and effortless the process will become.

You Only Communicate With Your Own Oversoul

You only communicate with your own Oversoul, and never with any other Oversoul. Whenever necessary, your Oversoul communicates with other Oversouls. Because all communication is filtered through one source, this method is very clean. Any information that you receive from your outer or inner worlds is always interpreted for your special needs.

Your Oversoul has complete knowledge of everything that you *need* to know, and communicates it back to you. This may be entirely different from what you *want* to know.

Explaining the outer world to you is the responsibility of your Oversoul. Collecting the data, passing it up, and interpreting the response are your responsibilities.

You Do Not Control

Through this method of communication, you do not control anyone. You only discuss something with your own Oversoul. It does the work for you.

For instance, you may decide to set up some experiments to determine if there is anything to this method of communication. You talk to your brother via the involved Oversouls, and he phones you to discuss exactly what you shared with him on the inner levels. You label this an interesting coincidence, and repeat the same experiment with a friend. Meeting him on the street, he also brings up the same things that you shared with him on the inner levels.

After several such incidents, you may begin to feel that *you* have the power to influence and control people. This is simply not so. It is your Oversoul that sets up the circumstances. If you take the credit instead of thanking your Oversoul for its help, these principles will stop working for you. Part of the responsibility for using these principles is recognizing that you alone have little power.

You can always tell your Oversoul what you do or do not want to happen. But because it has more knowledge, let it make the final decisions. Whatever your Oversoul allows to happen is always in your best interest. You may not always understand this, but as you objectively observe and ask questions, the reasons eventually become clear.

If you tell your Oversoul that you want a particular situation to occur regardless of the consequences, your Oversoul may allow it to happen so that you realize why it should not have happened.

Experiment On Your Own

Experiment on your own, and discover for yourself ways that your Oversoul can work with and for you. You are no longer alone. You are connecting with your true parent who wants to know you and your experiences.

FEELINGS

When you were a baby, you did not understand words, yet you still understood what was happening around you. You understood feelings, and you communicated through feelings.

When the people around you were upset, you understood and you became upset. If they were laughing and happy, you laughed and were happy right along with them. You knew when they were just saying "No!" and when they really *meant* "No!"

At this stage in your life, you were totally in touch with your feelings. You knew when you were hungry and you let everyone know. You knew when you were uncomfortable and you let them know that, too. You were communicating in a language without words.

Replacing Feelings With Words

Eventually, as you learned to talk, you stopped identifying the feelings and began identifying the words. You *replaced* your knowledge of feelings with words, instead of *supplementing* your knowledge of feelings with words.

For example, as an adult you do not always know when you are hungry. You eat for entertainment, for pacifying depression, from boredom, or just because it is time. As an adult you often do not even use the correct words to describe what you feel.

You may use the words, "I am hungry," but what you

really feel is, "I am bored. I would like some quick entertainment." You may even think that you are hungry.

You may use the words, "You make me angry," but what you really feel is frustration from a hard day at work. Not able to express your frustration during the day, you suppress that emotion. When you get home, you find yourself getting angry with your spouse or children. You think that they are frustrating you. You have lost touch with the origin of your feelings.

Identify Your Feelings

Because you are accustomed to communicating with words, you have lost touch with much of your sense of feeling. The feelings still occur, but you do not take the time to identify them as feelings. You move very quickly into the words that can only *try* to describe them.

All experience is feeling. Actually, feeling involves one or more of all five senses:

Taste—

Sweet and smooth are words that try to define what you feel when you eat.

Sight—

Beautiful and peaceful are words that try to define what you feel when you see.

Hearing—

Pitch and rhythm are words that try to define what you feel when you listen.

Touch—

Soft and rough are words that try to define what you feel when you touch.

Smell—

Fresh and clean are words that try to define what you feel when you breathe.

Each of the five senses must be experienced in order to know what the words mean. You can use all the words that you want, yet you can only try to describe what an orange tastes like to a person who has never tasted one.

Tasting an orange is an experience that produces feelings inside of your mouth. Sweet, juicy, cool, and clean can only *try* to describe its taste. The other person may get a general idea, but never knows what it actually tastes like without the experience.

Life Without Words

If there were no words to help define your outer world, you would still develop a way to communicate with yourself.

For instance, every time you touched something soft, you would remember the feeling. Every time that you touched something rough, you would remember *that* feeling. You would identify a sameness of all soft objects, and a sameness of all rough objects.

Eventually, you would recognize the differences between rough and soft by identifying the feelings you experienced each time you touched one or the other. Even without words, you would still communicate with yourself.

You almost always express yourself with words. Even when no one is around, you think in words. Now, you must go backwards through your words in order to touch into your feeling nature.

You Unconsciously React

You already feel many things without stopping to identify them. Unconsciously, you react to these feelings without allowing this information to filter through into your conscious mind.

For example, when you walk into any room in your home you are unconsciously aware of many details. When you walk into your living room you know who the people in your family are without stopping to consciously identify them. Every object in that room has a story behind it. You know that story without stopping to consciously think about it. Each story is an experience, and each story produces different feelings.

Your best friend gave you a plant for your birthday and glancing at it makes you feel pleasant. Your favorite aunt gave you one of her most treasured knick-knacks which does not fit your decor. Because she comes to visit often, you must keep it on display. You try to avoid looking at it.

But, both the plant and the knick-knack add to the atmosphere, or feeling, of the room.

Did you spend a wonderful evening last night with someone close? That feeling is still in the room when you walk in. Is there a fire in the fireplace? Colors, windows, books, stereos, paintings, and furniture all add to the feeling of the room.

Just by walking into your living room, you know all of this information in a split second by feeling it. Direct awareness gives you the knowledge. You know by knowing.

Slowing Down

On some level of awareness you react to all the feelings that your outer world is sending out. When you slow down long enough to feel these feelings, you can understand your reactions to any given situation.

For example, you have an important business meeting to attend. When you walk into the room, what feeling is projected in the room? Every place of business has its own feeling and usually reflects the personalities of the upper management. Is the room open and receptive? Does it have barriers? Is it cold? Just by walking into the room, you begin understanding the people with whom you will be doing business.

When you meet the people, what feelings are they projecting? Are they smiling and saying pleasant words, even though you feel anger and hostility in their auras? Is their anger and hostility directed at you? Or, is it at their supervisor, or family? And, are they directing those feelings at you because they need to clean out their anger? If so, how can you prepare yourself?

Their body language, clothing, and colors tell you who and what they are. These are reflections of their inner feelings.

Every person and object projects feelings. Slowing down allows you to feel whatever it is that your outer world is projecting. These feelings take you through the illusions into the reality of what is. This allows you to accurately interpret any given situation, and respond accordingly.

Understanding the feelings of your outer world helps you to understand the feelings of your inner world. Through direct awareness you learn that one always complements the other.

Cleaning Up Your Words

Observe your words to determine when they match what you feel inside and when they do not. If you are bored, do not say that you are hungry, say that you are bored. You confuse people when you say that you are hungry but really you are bored.

They hear your words, but on some level they feel their double meaning. Because they do not know how to label what they feel, they become uncomfortable.

When your words match what you feel, you are touching into your feeling nature. This is called "cleaning up your words." People will respond to the clarity of your words, and become more comfortable with you.

Cleaning up your words changes the reactions of other people to you. When you go home and state to your family, "I had a terribly frustrating day at work, and I feel frustrated!" you suddenly find the support that you have wanted for so many years. They react to the clarity of your words, and drop their defenses because they are no longer under attack. This teaches you to match feelings with feelings, and feelings with words.

Match Feelings With Feelings

As a child you were already matching feelings with feelings, but you have lost much of that skill. For example, you may have wanted milk to drink. Your desire for milk is a feeling (taste). Instead of milk, you said water, so that is what you were given. You immediately identified the taste as something other than milk.

Your memory of the milk taste did not match the water taste. You had to wait until someone gave you milk and repeated the word again. You had to match that taste with the memory of your taste with the word being spoken. Then, you had to remember the word "milk" so that you could ask for it the next time.

This process is very painstaking for a child, and consumes a lot of time and energy. Because you thought it was no longer necessary, you have forgotten this process of trial and error.

Getting back in touch with your feelings is an interesting challenge. You may have to reach into some areas of your life that you have been avoiding. You may feel uncomfortable, but that is okay. It is all part of the process. Remember, you already have the skill—it is just a bit rusty.

Your Oversoul Communicates Through Feeling

Your Oversoul communicates with you through feeling. You may receive pictures, symbols, sounds, words, and vibrations, but behind all of them is feeling. They direct your attention, but the knowing occurs when you accurately interpret the feeling behind them.

Using The Process Explains The Process

Many feelings are already coming forward from your inner world. Your willingness to acknowledge yourself automatically allows more information to surface into your conscious mind. This information comes in the form of feeling. Understanding the feeling tells you who you are.

Just as in meditation, using the process explains the

process. For example, during meditation you receive a picture of a woman on a covered wagon. When you are in touch with your feelings, you automatically know the meaning of this picture. There is a process that teaches you to understand the meaning of the picture within seconds.

Project that part of yourself that contains your feelings up into the channel that connects you to your Oversoul. Feel if the woman in the picture feels like you. If she does, then you are seeing yourself in a past lifetime. You match what you feel like with what she feels like. In the same way, you communicate with your Oversoul by asking questions and feeling the answers.

Through the process of trial and error, ask a question, feel an answer, and then project yourself up into the channel. If what you feel inside matches what you feel in the channel, you have your answer. If not, continue asking questions until both feelings match. For example:

What is the woman feeling on the covered wagon?

Is she exuberant and excited?

If you know what exuberance and excitement feel like, project up into the channel to feel for a match.

Is she exhausted and weary?

If you know what exhaustion and weariness feel like, feel that for a match.

Is she married?

What does being married feel like?

What does being single feel like?

Which feeling matches the way she feels?

Continue to ask questions and feel for matches until you know everything that you need to know about her:

How old she was:
  Does she feel like—
    a teenager?
    a middle-aged person?
    an old person?
    someone in her thirties? forties?

Where she came from:
  Does she feel like she came from—
    the East Coast?
    the Midwest?
    England?

If she had any children, and if so, how many:
  What does it feel like—
    not to have any children?
    to have one child?
    to have two children?
    to have six children?
    to have boys?
    to have girls?
    to have boys and girls?

If she was happy—
  What does feeling happy feel like?
  What does feeling unhappy feel like?

If she completed the trip, and why or why not—
  What does it feel like to complete a trip?
  What does it feel like not to complete a trip?

How long she lived—

Can you feel her at thirty, but not at forty?

Continue to ask questions and feel for matches. You can determine whatever your Oversoul wants you to know by understanding the feeling that is behind one picture. You "know by knowing" so many things from one picture, the same as you "know by knowing" when you walk into your living room.

Daily Guidance

In the same way, ask for daily guidance from your Oversoul. Continue the process of matching feelings with feelings, utilizing the clues to direct your learning. As an example, you decide to discuss something important with a friend and you are not sure if you should approach him/her now, or wait.

Ask your Oversoul if the timing is correct.

Project up through your thoughts into the channel that connects yourself to your Oversoul.

From past experience, remember what correct timing feels like—

The person reacted favorably.

The conversation went smoothly.

You felt satisfied that you got your point across.

(This set of experiences left a feeling inside of you).

From past experience, remember what incorrect timing feels like—

The person acted put out.

The conversation was awkward.

You knew that your time was wasted.

(This set of experiences left a feeling inside of you).

What are you feeling in the channel?

Does it match your memory of the feelings that correct timing produces?

Does it match your memory of the feelings that incorrect timing produces?

You think it matches your memory of the feelings that correct timing produces, so you decide to speak to your friend now.

You speak to your friend, and then you evaluate—

Did the person react favorably?

Did the conversation go smoothly?

Were you satisfied that you got your point across?

If you could answer yes to the above questions, then you correctly interpreted the communication from your Oversoul.

Remember this feeling so that you can repeat the experience and go through the steps faster.

If you answer no to the above questions, then you have direct knowledge of what it is like when you are not correctly interpreting the communication from your Oversoul.

It is just as important to know when you are not correctly interpreting the communication from your Oversoul.

This allows you to build a data base of both types of feelings.

You Have A Partner

What your Oversoul directs you to do may not always coincide with what you want. Your Oversoul is your partner, and because it is the one with the most knowledge, it always has the final say.

For example, you may want to gossip about someone, but your Oversoul directs you not to. If you gossip anyway, the power of your words will return to you with the same force that you sent them. Because you have more knowledge, you must balance your actions with wisdom. In other words, you are now more accountable for your actions.

You may want to spend your money one way, but your Oversoul tells you to spend it another way. You may want to dress for an occasion one way, and your Oversoul may direct you into different clothing.

The more that you work with your inner guidance, the easier it becomes to interpret it. As you learn to interpret it, you learn to trust it. What you were previously labeling "hunches" takes on new meaning.

Next, you may go through a period where you want to listen to your Oversoul, but you do not. This is because you may be told something that you do not want to hear.

When you pass through that stage, you listen, but do as you want anyway. During this time, you learn that had you listened in the first place, you would have been happier with the outcome. You may not always know why your Oversoul is directing you as it is, but if you observe and pay attention, the reasons eventually become clearer.

Move Upward Into Your Potential

This rebellion is normal. You are unaccustomed to this type of guidance. You are used to acting independently, even if you chose to give that independence to another person. You now give your independence to your Oversoul, knowing that it helps you to grow very quickly by pulling you upward into your potential.

Know By Knowing

The more you practice interpreting feelings, the more adept you become at understanding them. You know by knowing what you feel, what feelings other people and objects project, and what your Oversoul communicates to you.

You recognize and interpret a sizable amount of information in a split second, just by feeling. You know so much that it takes longer to articulate all that you know than it does to feel it. This is the same process that you go through every day when you walk into your living room.

All you have to do is recognize what you are already doing, label it, and then take the time to consciously repeat the experience at will. Whenever you understand feelings, you know by knowing. It is within this level that you have direct awareness.

The deeper that you touch into your feeling nature, the more you understand. Words are an essential form of communication, but as you move through them, you rediscover the importance of feeling.

RELEASING THE PAST

Every day brings new experiences into your life. Each experience teaches you something, whether you are aware of it or not. If you do not learn from an experience, you continue to have similar experiences until you learn whatever it is that you need to know.

All experiences have an effect upon you, whether you recognize this or not. After the experience is gone, the feeling of the experience remains with you. This feeling is vibration, and leaves an imprint in your personal energy field, or aura.

Your Aura Reflects Your Experiences

Your aura reflects your experiences through:

Color

Clarity

Symbols

Patterns

Flow

Smell

Rate of vibration

Vibratory Imprints Are Cumulative

You are individualized neutral energy with the vibrations

of your experiences circulating around you. As similar experiences are repeated, the feelings that are left are drawn to the "like" vibratory imprints that already exist within your aura and strengthen them. These vibratory imprints are cumulative—not only in this lifetime, but from one to another, and affect your mental and emotional state.

Every time you are angry, the experience leaves a feeling within you. These feelings pass into your body, then out into your aura. They are attracted to like vibratory imprints. Illusion tells you that the anger experience is over, but reality tells you that it is only out of your conscious mind.

On some level of awareness, you still feel and react to that anger experience, as well as to the cumulative ones that surround you. The more anger experiences you have, the stronger the vibratory imprint for anger becomes.

You react to your everyday experiences through these accumulated vibratory imprints. Because you react through them, any situation can easily make you angry.

For example, one of your children accidentally breaks a piece of your good china. It becomes an excuse to vent some of your accumulated anger. Then, you wonder why you got so angry, and you feel guilty. Because you have so much suppressed anger buried in your body and aura, you need some way to release it. This usually means that you try to clean out your pain by inflicting it on someone else.

Vibratory Imprints Affect the Body

Feelings create vibratory imprints. When vibratory imprints grow strong enough, they directly affect the physical body. They are something that can be seen and felt on some level of awareness. You actually manifest something, the same as you do when you put a bubble around your aura.

As they grow stronger, they become more dense and settle into your physical body. This effect can either be positive or negative, and you actually wear these vibratory imprints in your body. These vibratory imprints affect:

Your quality of health—

How well your body functions on a daily basis.

Any chronic illness.

Mannerisms—

How you talk, walk, gesture, carry yourself.

Tension—

If it is or is not present in your body.

If it is, where.

Your body is affected by all of the feelings that you have ever had.

Releasing Vibratory Imprints

Your aura and physical body can only contain a given number of vibratory imprints. Eventually, they become full, and the vibratory imprints must be released. There are five ways to release them:

Accidents

Illness

Words

Physical death

Consciously to your Oversoul

Accidents

The established vibratory imprints that surround you can become so thick and heavy that they must have some type of physical impact to release them. An accident quickly creates the impact that you need. It can be a major one, or perhaps only a bump on the head. An accident releases the patterns by breaking them up and dispersing them before they become so dense that they create a major illness in your body.

Illness

Illness rearranges the vibratory imprints that surround you. Fevers burn up and clean out vibratory imprints that are becoming dense. This releases them before they turn into a chronic illness. A chronic illness is the result of specific repeated negative behavior patterns.

Sometimes when you are working very hard to make changes, you may cause a minor illness because you are releasing the toxins that negative feelings have left behind. You feel their effects on their way out of your body.

Because body, mind, and spirit are all interconnected, it does not matter which spoke on the wheel gets rearranged. One always directly affects the other. Rearranging the biological structure of the body through illness changes something in your mental, emotional, and/or spiritual bodies.

Words

Words provide a quick and easy release for your vibratory imprints. When an especially happy or upsetting event occurs, for instance, you cannot wait to tell someone about it. Your thoughts are energy, and speaking them releases some of this energy. You feel it go.

This is especially easy to demonstrate when you are angry. You feel the anger well up in your solar plexus, or stomach area. You feel it come right up your throat and out of your mouth. When you are through speaking, you feel drained.

You have cleaned yourself out. Unfortunately, you have only put those anger feelings out into the air. Because they are a part of you, they eventually come back to you. Anger going out means anger coming back.

Physical Death

Eventually, even with accidents, illness, and spoken words, your aura and body become full. Your body dies, and you go directly to your Oversoul to release the vibratory imprints of your accumulated past experiences if your Oversoul wants them. Together, you review your life: what you learned and what still needs to be learned. You decide which experiences are completed and which ones are not.

Your Oversoul may take all of your experiences, some of them, or none of them. Perhaps the contract that you agreed upon before you were born determined that you would go several lifetimes before you would release them to your Oversoul.

Conscious Release

The last way to clean out vibratory imprints is to consciously release them up to your Oversoul. When you consciously release them, you do not have to carry the feelings that they have left within and around you. Releasing negative patterns means that you no longer have to wear them in your body or aura.

It is also important to release positive vibratory imprints, because they too are the result of leftover feelings from past experiences. You need the space around you as clear and clean as possible.

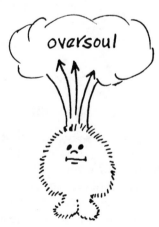

Your Aura And Body Reflect Your Work

As you release in conscious awareness, your aura and body reflect the work that you are doing.

Your aura—

Changes color.

Becomes clearer.

Becomes less dense.

Changes symbols and patterns.

Smells cleaner.

Flows smoother and more evenly.

Quickens its rate of vibration.

Your physical body—

Looks younger.

Functions more efficiently on a daily basis.

Releases its tension.

Changes its mannerisms.

Begins healing any chronic illness.

Cleaning Yourself Up

You might compare yourself to a child that has never had a bath. It is possible to wash away the dirt that has accumulated not only in this lifetime, but also in others. Consciously releasing vibratory imprints allows you to remove the feelings that past experiences have left in your body and aura that are no longer necessary.

This cleaning process allows you to evaluate your life more clearly. You no longer have to view it through the feelings of past experiences. Because you are less agitated by vibratory imprints that are not calm and peaceful, you automatically become calmer and more peaceful.

It becomes easier to walk through the turmoil of the outer world without being pulled into it. While remaining centered and balanced, you can objectively observe whatever is happening around you. With less agitation to pull you outward, you also will find it easier to go into deeper levels of inner awareness during meditation.

Release Daily Experiences

To keep vibratory imprints from accumulating, release daily experiences to your Oversoul as they occur. This releasing process allows you to review your daily activities, and evaluate:

What you learned.

What still needs to be learned.

How you can learn it.

With the permission and guidance of your Oversoul, make changes in your life moment by moment, day by day. Become a conscious partner in your personal development and spiritual growth.

Pleasant Experiences

Releasing daily activities is not always as easy as it sounds, and is a skill that must be developed. It does not matter if the experience is positive or negative. You may not want to let go of pleasant experiences because you think that they are too far and few between. You may want to hold onto them until you are certain that you will have another one.

Conflict

Surprisingly, you even want to hold onto conflict. Conflict has always played an important role and has been a wonderful teacher and entertainer. If you release known events, you must replace them with unknown events. Replacing conflict with an unknown can be very scary.

After eons of learning through conflict, there may be a part of you that does not want to give it up. This part has worked long and hard through many lifetimes to gain experience from that conflict. Explain to that part of yourself that you appreciate its knowledge, but your Oversoul needs the information that it contains. Tell it that if you need to contact it, you will do so through your Oversoul.

The Past

As you become competent in releasing daily activities, experiences and feelings from your past start coming forward into your conscious mind. Release everything up to your Oversoul, observing it as it passes out of you. Any experience that still causes a strong reaction from you is not finished.

Will yourself into your center, and let the part of you that still reacts complete that experience. Let it feel any emotion that it wants to, and express itself accordingly. Release those feelings up the channel to your Oversoul. When you are ready to totally release the experience, you can identify both the positive and negative aspects of it. You feel neutral toward the experience.

Sometimes your illusions may tell you that you feel neutral toward an experience. The reality may be that you are ignoring some negative aspects. Be sure to examine every corner of yourself. In order to clean yourself out, you must acknowledge what exists within you.

Past Lives

As you cleanse yourself, experiences from past lives may also begin to come forward into your conscious mind. Release these on up to your Oversoul and ask for an explanation. Ask your Oversoul to explain why this particular life is being shown to you and what significance it has on your present.

If you do not receive an explanation, do not keep the experience but release it back up until you receive one. In order to move deeper into the level of knowing by knowing, you must release the level that teaches you to know by guessing. Trust that what you need to know will be explained when it has relevance to you.

Focus On The Present

Because you no longer react as intensely through your past experiences, it becomes easier to focus on the present moment. You react to the present, rather than to memories of past experiences. You have a better understanding of why you are doing what you are doing, when you are doing it. You learn from and appreciate the present moment.

Using The Process

Only by releasing everything to your Oversoul can you be cleansed. This process allows you to view your life from a more objective perspective. The more objective you can be, the more accurate your evaluations. Then you can identify specific patterns of behavior, and make conscious decisions on what and how to change.

The releasing process continues to build your connections with universal energy. It moves your energy up and down, and strengthens your communication with your Oversoul. As you use the process, you learn about the process. And, the process continues to teach you through direct awareness.

GROWING YOUNGER

People age at an artificially accelerated rate. On some level of awareness people automatically assume that they will grow old, and deteriorate mentally and physically. The collective unconscious tells them that they will grow old and deteriorate.

Many people exercise and watch their diet, but there is one more factor to maintaining youth. The physical body is also a creation of vibratory imprints.

The Body Is A Parable

The physical body is a reflection of past experiences. For example, you can interpret the lifetime experiences of people by observing them. Their faces may be smiling, but the lines on them, the roundness of shoulders, and the heaviness of walk all tell in parable the stories of their lives.

Their bodies tell you that life has not always been easy, and that they have struggled through pain and conflict. They can also tell you specific experiences and feelings. Their bodies carry the weight of their vibratory imprints.

Because these vibratory imprints are cumulative, often by the time people are in their twenties, their bodies already show signs of aging. Their mannerisms and facial expressions reflect the struggles of childhood and early adult years. They may have a little extra weight, which reflects the extra mental baggage, or vibratory imprints, that they carry with them. Or, they may look rigid and tense from the density of their vibratory imprints.

As each decade rolls by and more vibratory imprints accumulate, the aging process speeds up. Your body continues to be a parable that tells you and others about your past experiences. You carry all of the leftover feelings of your past experiences with you, and it can be a heavy burden.

You Do Not Have To Carry The Weight Of Your Past

It is possible to have the knowledge of your past actions without carrying the effects of their vibratory imprints with you. You can release your feelings from your experiences, as they occur, up to your Oversoul. This releases them from your aura and keeps it clear and clean. Your body does not have to reflect your life experiences. You do not have to carry the weight of your past with you.

Your Oversoul is waiting for your experiences. It wants to know:

What you experienced.

How you reacted.

How other people reacted.

What emotions you felt.

Rather than wait to tell your Oversoul at the end of your life, consciously release all of that information now.

Visualize Your Oversoul As A Cloud

Your Oversoul is neutral energy. Because at this point you do not know exactly what this energy looks like, or even if you have an Oversoul, experiment with some of the following principles to determine their validity.

Visualize your Oversoul as a white, fluffy cloud above your head, connected by a clear, elasticized channel. To release your experiences, send your thoughts, feelings, and pictures up this channel. Watch them disappear into the cloud, and observe that the cloud always stays clean.

Release Your Feelings

Release all of the feelings from your experiences at the end of each day. Trying to hold onto them may cause sleeplessness. In some instances negative feelings can keep you awake by providing hours of entertainment. Holding onto positive feelings helps prolong positive experiences.

The feelings from daily experiences settle into the physical body fairly quickly. A cramp in your leg at night, for example, reminds you of the fun that you had on a hike. A headache reminds you of the tension of the day. Both are examples of how quickly vibratory imprints settle into the body.

Take a few minutes each morning to release your learning from the night. All kinds of learning occur while you sleep. On some level of awareness your night learning also produces feelings that accumulate in your aura.

Keep Cleaning

The most efficient way to keep yourself clean is to release the feelings of any experience as it occurs. All you have to do is feel and/or watch your feelings pass up the channel to your Oversoul.

If you forget to release them, ask your Oversoul to clean up your leftover feelings from the past week, month, year, or years. Feel and watch them leave your body and aura en masse.

You do not have to go into a meditative state to clean. Start right now by stopping for a couple of minutes, and will the cleaning to begin. Clean yourself up anytime you happen to think about it—while watching television, doing laundry, driving, or even exercising.

Cleaning actually releases something from yourself. These leftover feelings which comprise your vibratory imprints are a creation of your thoughts, and have weight. They are dark and heavy, and usually muddy brown or black. Watch them go up the channel, and feel how much lighter and cleaner you are.

Continue cleaning any time that you happen to think about it. Because your vibratory imprints have accumulated over a long period of time, you most likely will not release them all at once. It takes time to effectively clean yourself out.

Strong Vibratory Imprints

When you have had many, many similar experiences, the vibratory imprints that result from them are very strong. Some are so strong, they almost seem to have a will of their own. No matter how many times you try to release them up to your Oversoul, they never seem to weaken. These vibratory imprints have been fed very well from your leftover feelings. In a sense, they have become a type of life form. They are a part of you, yet separate from you.

Now, all of a sudden, you are telling your creation to remove itself from your life. Naturally, it does not want to leave and it is going to protest. Releasing it from your space means that it must venture into the unknown and it does not want to go. It thinks that you are trying to destroy it and it tries to hang on harder.

Call up this part of yourself, either during meditation, or whenever you have a quiet moment to yourself. Visualize it as an image of yourself talking to the you that is in your center. Ask this image why it does not want to go. Allow it to talk and talk until it is out of words and is exhausted.

Thank it for sharing itself and explain that it is important. You appreciate it and all that it has gone through to acquire its knowledge. However, your Oversoul now wants it. Whenever you need any information that it has, you will communicate with it through your Oversoul.

Visualize yourself handing this part of you up through the channel and into the cloud that represents your Oversoul. If it comes back, repeat this procedure. Continue to hand it back to your Oversoul.

Working With Negative Emotions

This method is especially useful when working with

116

negative emotions. For instance, if you want to remove the vibratory imprint of anger from your aura, you are going to discover that many experiences have contributed to that imprint.

When you release it up, it may keep returning. Visualize this angry part of yourself, and ask it why it is angry. Allow it to tell you, while you stay in your center as the objective observer. When it is through, thank it, and release it up to your Oversoul.

Removing Blocks

This method is helpful for removing blocks of any kind. Say you do not like to balance your checkbook, but you want to start balancing it. Call up the part of you that does not like this activity, and ask it to explain why. Let it talk, do not try to suppress it, and listen. You may be surprised at what it tells you. Seemingly unrelated events may surface that you had forgotten about long ago. These events can be cleaned up by releasing them, and you can finally keep your checkbook balanced.

Positive And Negative Aspects

When a vibratory imprint is finally weakened enough to move completely out of your aura, you will be aware of both the positive and negative aspects of the experiences that have produced your feelings. For example, you will know all of the positive and negative aspects of not keeping your checkbook balanced.

Some of the positive aspects are:

You do not have to worry about the amount of money in your checking account since you do not know how much it is.

You provide another reason to argue with your spouse, allowing you to clean out pent-up frustrations.

You have more time for things that you really enjoy.

Some of the negative aspects are:

Because you do not know how much money you have, you do not know how much you can spend.

You wish you did not have so many arguments with your spouse so that you could feel closer.

You feel guilty when you do not have an accurate checkbook balance, because with a little effort, you know that you could.

Releasing Excess Aura Weight

Not all vibratory imprints can be released at once. But, you can begin to break them up and release them from your aura. You feel calmer and more peaceful as you release this excess baggage. The weight released from your aura will be reflected in your body, regardless of your chronological years.

If you have ever gained and lost weight, it is much the same feeling. You can easily put on ten pounds without realizing that you have gained any weight. Have you ever looked at a ten pound sack of flour in the grocery store and wondered what it would be like to have it strapped to your back all day? It would be quite a weight to carry.

So, how could you put on ten pounds and not notice it? It is not until you actually take off those ten pounds that you realize how sluggish you felt with the extra weight. It is the same with your accumulated vibratory imprints. You do not realize their weight and effects until you take them off, or in this case, release them up to your Oversoul.

Keep Yourself Strong And Solid

Not only do you carry the leftover feelings of your experiences, but you have scattered your feelings all around you. The impact from the accidents that you have had, the words that you have spoken, material objects that you have created and/or touched, and even your thoughts, have dispersed your vibratory imprints from your aura. You want your feelings gathered in one place to keep you as strong and solid as possible.

Ask your Oversoul to pull all your feelings in from any place that you have been during the day. If you do not, then other people will react to the thoughts and feelings that you have left behind. Visualize a giant vacuum cleaner sucking up all of the vibrations that you left, and then watch them disappear into the cloud that is your Oversoul.

Do Not Scatter Yourself

Once your vibratory imprints have been pulled into your Oversoul, do your best to keep from scattering yourself. You can ask that your feelings be cleaned up and released to your Oversoul on an event-by-event basis, or daily, weekly, or even yearly. However, the sooner that you get pulled back into yourself, the stronger and more solid you will be.

Distinguish What Is Yours

The releasing process teaches you through direct awareness that there are many areas in your life which you think are yours and yours alone, but which are not. Just as you have scattered your feelings wherever you have been, other people have also scattered themselves around you. Why deal with their feelings and frustrations when you have enough of your own?

For example, not all of the feelings in your home are yours. You not only react through the accumulated feelings of your past experiences, you also react to the thoughts and feelings that other people have unconsciously dumped in your home.

On some level, you react to the feelings that previous owners and their guests have left. You react to the feelings of the people who manufactured the furniture in your home and who produced the food in your refrigerator. Every time someone touches something, they leave a bit of themselves behind.

The reason that mom's home cooking tastes so good, for example, is not always because she is such a wonderful cook. Not only do you eat the food that she has prepared, you also ingest the feelings behind the food. You feel the time and care that she spent planning, purchasing, and preparing it. She not only nourishes you with the food that you see with your physical eyes, she also nourishes you with her care.

But, when you ingest her care, you also ingest whatever feelings she attaches to her care. It may be a concern for you, a fear that you are not happy, or a frustration that she cannot do more for you. You do not want those feelings in you.

For this reason it is important to distinguish what is yours and what is not. Ask your Oversoul to bless the food and release any feelings that are not yours. Ask that those feelings be cleaned up and returned to their rightful owner. Your Oversoul will take care of the logistics. This continues to keep you clean and clear.

Clean Up As Much As Possible

Cleaning up as many experiences as possible means that you only deal with you. Allow other people to have what is rightfully theirs and keep only what is yours. You cannot mix others' feelings with yours if you want to find out who you are.

The following is a list to help you get started with the cleaning process:

Conversations—

Ask that the energy of your words be cleaned up and returned to your Oversoul.

Ask that any misunderstandings be clarified through the involved Oversouls.

Relationships—

Ask that they be cleaned up, explained, and the knowledge returned to you.

Health—

Ask that your body be cleaned up and strengthened so

that it can provide the most efficient home for you while you are here.

Finances—

Ask that your feelings be released from any money that you spend.

Give thanks that it has been provided for you, and let go of it with appreciation.

Home—

Ask that any feelings in your home that do not belong to you be cleaned up and returned to their rightful owners.

When you have had visitors, ask that their feelings be cleaned up and returned to them.

Possessions—

All of your possessions have been handled by many people who have all left some of their feelings on them.

Ask that they be cleaned up, and any feelings that are not yours be returned to their rightful owners.

Food—

Ask that any food that you eat be blessed, cleaned up, and the feelings of others be returned to their rightful owners.

Bodily waste—

It also contains your vibrations.

Ask that your vibrations be returned to your Oversoul, and the physical waste continue on its journey.

Anything that you give away or sell—

Ask that your vibrations be returned to your Oversoul.

Ask that it be cleaned up and made ready for its new owner, whomever that might be.

When you stop and put labels on all the feelings that you carry with you, you understand why your body ages so quickly.

Your Psychic Energy

Cleaning yourself up and releasing the excess weight of vibratory imprints allows your personal, or psychic energy to flow with less constraints.

With age, the psychic energy slows down because it must constantly push through all of the accumulated vibratory imprints that have settled into the body. For example, your body cannot always effectively use the food that you feed it because the psychic energy which controls the digestive juices gets bogged down with the weight of your vibratory imprints.

The entire system is thrown out of balance when the energy that has been provided for it cannot be fully utilized. As unnecessary vibratory imprints are released, psychic energy flows more freely through the body. It can do what it needs to do, and as a result, the body functions much more efficiently.

Slowing Down The Aging Process

You can slow down the aging process by taking a few minutes every day to release some of your leftover feelings. Your chronological age does not matter. Cleaning out your vibratory imprints lightens your aura and pulls an amazing amount of weight off of your physical body.

One day, you will look in the mirror, and realize that you do look younger and more vibrant. Your skin has better color and your face and body look more relaxed. This encourages you to continue releasing, which in turn allows you to build a stronger, healthier body, regardless of your chronological age.

Love Your Body

When you look at your body in the mirror, take a moment to love it. Realize that you created whatever it is that your body is expressing. Instead of ignoring, chastising, or criticizing the parts that you do not like, or do not think work the way that they "should", tell them that you love them.

Remember, your body is a product of your own thoughts, and is proof of the power that you hold. What you do with that power is always your choice. It is your decision whether you use it to tear your body down or to build a strong and healthy one.

YOU ARE LIMITLESS

You are discovering that all of your answers are within and around you. You are recognizing and utilizing the clues that take you into these answers. Using your answers, you are moving into continually deeper levels of inner awareness.

You are finding out how much you already know. All you are doing differently is slowing yourself down long enough to recognize what you know. Then, you are labeling and defining it so that you can repeat the process at will.

Your Reactions Are Changing

Your inner and outer worlds are the same as before you started this book, but now you are viewing them from a different perspective. This changes your reaction to them, and, in turn, their reaction to you.

Activating Inner Healing

Being aware of who and what you are automatically activates your inner healing process. Through direct awareness, you "know by knowing" that you can:

Find your own answers.

Define yourself.

Accept who you are.

Like who you are.

Clean up your past.

Take responsibility for yourself and your life.

Lay out the patterns for your future.

Make a difference in your inner and outer worlds.

Define spirituality and God.

Validate Your Information

This book has acted as a catalyst to move you into deeper levels of inner awareness. It is only a beginning point to give you direction. This book did not do the work, or give you experience. It has been up to you to validate the information and to determine what works and what does not.

There are many avenues of action, and just as many interpretations of those avenues. Always validate knowledge for yourself. Never be satisfied to say:

I read it in a book, so it must be true.

Someone told me, so it must be true.

You are becoming a scientist who gathers data, experiments with it, asks questions, and continually reevaluates it until you can say:

I know through direct awareness.

I know because I experienced it—

This is what did or did not happen.

I know by knowing.

Being aware of the tools that can take you into the knowledge is a beginning point. But, only when you have used them to gather your own data and applied it, is that knowledge truly yours. When you understand what you have learned by experiencing and feeling it, then you can say, "I know by knowing".

Be Open And Honest

Always ask your Oversoul and God to direct your learning. Be willing to move into deeper levels of inner awareness. This can only be accomplished when you are open and honest with yourself.

Grow Step By Step

Allow your life to grow in an orderly manner, step by step. Once you learn how to use one set of tools, the doors will open a little wider. Another set of tools will be waiting to take you into even deeper levels of inner awareness.

Through direct awareness, you know by knowing that you are infinitely deep, with an infinite well of answers. You already had the knowledge, and now you have some tools to help you access that knowledge.

Always be willing to move; to be open and receptive to growth and change. Never set limits for yourself; you might reach them and stay there. Set goals, and use them as significant events, continuing to recognize that you truly are limitless.

Good luck on your journey—
Janet Dian

APPENDICES

SOME
THINGS
TO
TRY

RING ON A STRING I

Demonstrate the power of your mind—
   Attach a piece of string to a ring.
   Hold the string between your thumb and forefingers.
   Steady your arm.
   With your thoughts, will the ring to move in a circle.
   It may take a few seconds before it actually moves.

Once it does, you can will it to—
   Move in larger or smaller circles.
   Change directions.
   Go back and forth.

RING ON A STRING II

Keep your arm steady—

Hold the ring above someone else's head, in the space that contains his/her thoughts.

Ask him/her to will the ring to move.

Observe what happens.

Try this—

Above a woman's head.

Above a man's head.

Observe the differences.

PROSPERITY

Allow yourself to feel prosperous—
    Carry a $50 or $100 bill in your wallet.
    Observe how prosperous it makes you feel.
    If you spend it, replace it as soon as you can.

CREATE A BUBBLE

Using the power of your thoughts, pull your aura in close to your body.

Create a clear bubble around it by taking a second or two to visualize one there.

You can make it as thick as you want to.

Evaluate your feelings—

Are you less tired around groups of people with it than without it?

Does it affect your ability to communicate?

ALL EXPERIENCES TEACH

Think of an experience that caused you pain, misery, suffering, and/or discomfort:

List the perks.

List the growth that it has brought you:

What it taught you about your own capabilities—

Your strengths.

Your weaknesses.

Your potential.

What it taught you about other people.

FEEL THE SAMENESS
AND DIFFERENCES

Practice feeling and identifying the feelings of sameness and differences:

Feel the sameness of all—

Schools

Hospitals

Grocery stores

Government agencies

Funeral homes

Once you can feel the sameness of each group, then feel the differences between each group.

FEEL YOUR HOME

Your home has a unique feeling.

Feel how your home feels different from anyone else's home:

Stop and feel the colors that you have chosen—

How do they make you feel?

How are they reflective of your personality?

Are they:

bright and cheery?

warm and cozy?

soft and peaceful?

cold and hard?

dark and gloomy?

What feelings does your furniture project?

How do you feel about the windows and lighting in your home?

Does your home feel cluttered?

Does your home feel like you?

Does your home feel like your family?

Does one room feel more like one person than another?

What feelings do your personal belongings project?

How do you feel when you hold specific objects?

Do you have things in your home that you do not particularly like? If so, why do you keep them? Is it time to clean them out?

Continue asking questions that allow you to feel your home.

FEEL YOUR BODY

Is it possible that your body is full of leftover feelings from past experiences that you no longer need?

How would it feel if it did not contain leftover feelings?

FEEL ADVERTISEMENTS

When reading a newspaper or magazine, stop and feel the differences that each ad projects.

Each ad contains the feelings of the company that it came from.

Ask yourself the following questions as you feel the ads:

What does the ad convey about the feeling of the company?

Is it a company that you would want to do business with?

Why do you choose one company over another?

Do the ads of similar businesses have similar feelings?

SPEAK THROUGH YOUR OVERSOUL

Before you speak to anyone, address that person first through your Oversoul:

Explain what you want to talk about and why—

When you do talk to him/her, observe if he/she is any more receptive than usual.

Notice if that person brings up any of your concerns before you do.

• • •

Think of a situation or person that you have been avoiding:

Talk to the involved persons through your Oversoul.

Verbally speak to those persons.

Observe their reaction:

Do you think it is any different than if you had not prepared them through your Oversoul?

• • •

Collect your data:

Observe when you think that communicating through your Oversoul makes a difference and when you do not.

AFFIRMATIONS

AFFIRMATIONS

The following affirmations are short, simple, and easy to use. Choose one or two to think or say throughout your day. You might even like to write them. Expand or change them any way that personalizes them for you.

ACCEPTING YOUR BODY

I accept my body.

I appreciate my body.

I ask my Oversoul and God to bless my body.

I give thanks for my body.

I love my body.

I love (any part of your body that you don't like).

I love (any part of your body that doesn't work the way you think it "should").

ACCEPTING YOURSELF

I am willing to stop hiding from myself.

I accept my dual nature.

I learn from my positive and negative aspects.

I learn from my positive and negative experiences.

All my experiences teach me.

I am gentle with myself.

I accept my own self-worth.

I accept myself as I am.

APPRECIATION

I give thanks to my Oversoul and God for directing my inner learning.

I give thanks to my Oversoul and God for the knowledge, and for the wisdom to use it wisely.

I give thanks to my Oversoul and God for all that I have and all that I receive.

CONSCIOUS AWARENESS

I act in conscious awareness.

My energy flows up and down.

Whatever I need to know comes forward into my conscious mind.

I am able to find my own answers with the help of my Oversoul and God.

CONSCIOUS RELEASE

I consciously release my life to my Oversoul and God.

I release any feelings and experiences that I no longer need.

I am able to release my pleasant experiences.

I release my pleasant experiences to make room for more.

I am able to release my unpleasant experiences.

I no longer need to learn in a negative way.

I am willing to release my past.

I am willing to release any blocks that keep me from moving forward.

FEELINGS

I understand my feelings.

I am willing to identify the origin of my feelings.

I identify the origin of my feelings.

I am able to accurately feel what I need to know.

I feel whatever I need to know.

INNER AWARENESS

I move into continually deeper levels of inner awareness.

I know by knowing.

I know through direct awareness.

I acknowledge my limitlessness.

I accept my limitlessness.

INNER HEALING

I am willing to grow step by step.

I am responsible for my own inner healing.

I activate my own inner healing.

I take responsibility for my life.

I ask my Oversoul and God to direct me in my inner healing.

MEDITATION

I am able to sit quietly.

I am able to go deep within my center.

I enjoy my meditation time.

I objectively observe myself without judgment or criticism.

I feel the oneness with all that is.

I feel the expansion of myself beyond my body.

I feel the natural rhythm of the universe as it expands and contracts.

I am able to learn through direct awareness.

PRESENT MOMENT

I slow down and learn from my present moment.

I enjoy my present moment.

My present moment teaches me about me.

My present moment teaches me about my Oversoul.

My present moment teaches me about God.

MEDITATIONS
TO
GET
YOU
STARTED

SITTING QUIETLY I

If sitting quietly is difficult for you, try the following for five minutes for a few days:

Gently bend and stretch to release any tension that is present in your body.

Sit outside or at a window with your eyes open.

Observe your surroundings and think about the following questions—

Do you enjoy what you are looking at?

What things change from day to day?

What things stay the same?

Does the air have any particular feel or smell?

What emotions are you feeling?

Do you enjoy spending five minutes just sitting?

Observe your body and think about these questions—

Is it able to sit quietly for five minutes?

Does it enjoy the time, or does it feel agitated?

Is there tension in any part of it?

What parts are more relaxed than other parts?

Do not criticize or judge any thoughts or feelings that you have.

Merely observe what is occurring within you and your body.

SITTING QUIETLY II

Once you can sit quietly with your eyes open, then try the following for five minutes for a few days:

Gently bend and stretch to release any tension that is present in your body.

Sit in a comfortable chair that allows your spine to be straight.

Place your feet flat on the floor.

Place your hands in your lap, palm up in a receptive position.

Close your eyes.

Observe the emotions that you feel, and ask yourself the following questions—

Do I feel comfortable or uncomfortable?

Do I feel calm inside?

Do I enjoy sitting quietly?

Observe how your body feels, and ask yourself these questions—

Does it feel comfortable, or does it feel agitated?

Is it holding tension?

If it is, release it by willing the muscles holding the tension to relax.

Does it enjoy sitting quietly?

Do not criticize or judge any thoughts or feelings that you have.

Merely observe what is occurring within you and your body.

MEDITATION PRAYER

If you feel comfortable doing so, begin and end your meditation time with a prayer.

For example—

Divine Mother, Holy Father;

Thank you for preparing me for this meditation time. I am receptive to all that you wish to teach me.

• • •

Divine Mother, Holy Father;

Thank you for all that I learned during my meditation time. In your name, I give thanks. Amen.

FEELING THE DIFFERENCES

During meditation, feel the differences in the substances that your breath passes through.

As you breathe in and out—

Feel your breath pass through your physical body.

Feel your breath move into the space above your head that contains your thoughts.

Visualize and/or feel how far this space extends outward and upward.

Visualize and/or feel its shape and density.

Then, going beyond these limits, feel your breath move into the channel that connects you to your Oversoul.

Visualize and/or feel the space inside your channel.

When you look and feel beneath you, see and feel the space that holds your thoughts.

When you look and feel above you, see and feel the channel extending up toward your Oversoul.

Feel how the space in your channel feels different from the space that contains your thoughts.

Remember that feeling so that you can move into the channel whenever you wish.

Release your feelings up to your Oversoul, and complete your meditation.

MOVING INTO SILENCE

Follow your breath into deeper levels of inner awareness—

Use the word "silence".

As you breathe in from the top of your head to the base of your spine, think to yourself, "si-

As you breathe out from the base of your spine through the top of your head, think to yourself, -lence".

Feel yourself sink into deeper and deeper levels of inner peace and calm.

Recognize that you are touching into silence, the level of feeling.

Allow yourself to feel, even if you touch into it for just a few seconds.

This provides the trail that you will follow into deeper levels of inner awareness.

Release your feelings up to your Oversoul.

Complete your meditation.

EVENING RELEASING PRAYER

After following your breath into your center, personalize this prayer any way you wish—

Divine Mother, Holy Father:

Thank you for all that I have and all that I receive mentally, emotionally, physically, and spiritually. I thank you for the day, and for all the conscious and unconscious learning that it contained. Because it came from you, I give it back to you. If any part of the day needs further evaluation, let it pass before my inner eye.

[Visualize the activities of the day, dividing it into easy review form—

Morning; afternoon; evening; significant events.

Watch all of it pass out the top of your head, back up to your Oversoul. If anything is brought to your attention, give it further review as an objective observer. If not, give thanks for the learning of the day. You may do any other meditation work at this time.)]

I ask that you prepare me for tomorrow and all the lessons that it contains. I also ask that you prepare the people and the events that will be in my life tomorrow.

(You may want to mention any specific people and/or events.)

In your name, I give thanks. Amen.

MORNING RELEASING PRAYER

After following your breath into your center, personalize this prayer any way you wish—

Divine Mother, Holy Father:

Thank you for all conscious and unconscious learning that occurred within me during the night. If there is anything that you wish me to review, I ask that it pass before my inner eye.

[Review your dreams or any other occurrences from the night as an objective observer. Pass anything that you review out the top of your head and on up to your Oversoul.]

I return to you what came from you. In your name, I give thanks. Amen.

TRACING YOUR FEELINGS

Choose a situation in your life that is giving you problems. Let it pass before your inner eye and observe your reactions. Trace whatever emotions you feel back to their point of origin.

Release all of your feelings up to your Oversoul, labeling them as you go. Determine if you are reacting to the current situation or to something else.

For example, if your home life is unhappy, is this only because your job frustrates you? If so, what keeps you from making changes?

Is it—

fear?

low self-esteem?

lack of motivation?

because you do not feel you are good enough for or deserve another job?

After answering these questions, then decide how you need to change.

Your home life will reflect any inner changes that you make. Before it can change, you must go through these preliminary steps.

Identify what you feel and where those feelings come from. You cannot successfully change your home life if it is your job that needs changing first.

GLOSSARY

GLOSSARY

AURA: Your personal energy field.

AFFIRMATION: A statement in the present tense that defines a course of action, or a state of inner being. It is repeated many times by thinking, speaking, or writing it to bring new avenues of action into your conscious mind.

CENTER: Your center is aligned along your spine. It provides a safe space from which to work. You pull yourself into it by willing yourself into it.

COLLECTIVE UNCONSCIOUS: The body of space that contains the accumulated thoughts of humankind. These established thought patterns directly affect what you are moving through today.

CONSCIOUS MIND: Contains your present.

DIRECT AWARENESS: To know by experiencing the knowledge.

GOD: Neutral energy. All that is.

ILLUSION: The way you perceive things to be.

KNOW BY KNOWING: To know through direct awareness. To understand the feeling of an experience.

KNOWLEDGE: Information.

MACROCOSM: God. The universe.

MEDITATION: A process that moves you beyond words and connects you with silence, the level of feeling.

MICROCOSM: You. A world in miniature.

NEGATIVE: Negative is not "bad." It is merely a condition that exists.

OBJECTIVE OBSERVING: Watching and evaluating without judgment or criticism.

OVERSOUL: Neutral energy that comes out of God. Your Oversoul is to you what your Earth parents are to your body.

PSYCHIC ENERGY: Your personal energy. It flows back and forth and is horizontal.

POSITIVE: Positive is not better than negative. It is merely a condition that exists.

REALITY: The way things really are. It may vary considerably from your perception of the way you think things are.

SILENCE: The deepest level of inner awareness. The level of feeling. You connect with your Oversoul and God within silence.

SPIRITUALITY: A state of inner being.

SUBCONSCIOUS MIND: Contains your memories, moment by moment, lifetime by lifetime.

SUPERCONSCIOUS MIND: Provides the direct link to your Oversoul and God.

UNIVERSAL ENERGY: Energy that is available to everyone. Using it allows you to keep your psychic energy. It flows up and down and is vertical.

VIBRATORY IMPRINT: Accumulated feelings of like experiences. They cause you to react to your experiences of today through your accumulated feelings of yesterday.

WISDOM: Knowledge applied.

YOU: Individualized neutral energy.

INDEX

INDEX

C

D

ORDERING INFORMATION

For additional copies of

IN SEARCH OF YOURSELF: The Beginning

or

IN SEARCH OF YOURSELF: Moving Forward

please enclose $10.00 per book plus $1.50 shipping and handling for the first book and $1.00 shipping and handling for each additional book within the continental U.S.A.

International orders enclose $2.00 shipping and handling book rate (allow 8-10 weeks delivery) or $5.00 shipping and handling air mail.

Washington state residents add .075 sales tax.
All prices U.S. currency.

Send orders to:

Expansions Publishing Company, Inc.
609 W Washington
Suite 11-54   26
Sequim WA 98382

Allow 2-4 weeks for delivery.

Notes

Notes

Notes

Notes

Notes